Follow Your Heart

The Map To Illumination

By Puran and Susanna Bair

Living Heart Media
Tucson, AZ

Follow Your Heart: The Map To Illumination

Living Heart Media
PO Box 86149
Tucson AZ 85754
www.livingheartmedia.com

First edition

Printed in the United States of America

Edition ISBNs:

Softcover	978-0-9833038-0-0
Audio	978-0-9833038-2-4
E-Book	978-0-9833038-1-7

Table of Contents

List of Figures

Dedication

To Pir Vilayat Inayat Khan

Acknowledgments

We would like to acknowledge those whose generosity helped make this book possible:

Robin and Jack Carpenter
Helen Langlois Claire
Marybeth Guerrieri
Aliya Sabiha Malik
Steve and Kristy Olson
Jeanie Underwood
Porter Underwood

Thank you to those who contributed to the content of this book: Asatar Bair, Elijah Imlay, Paula Roome, Judith Simpson, Elizabeth Smith and other participants of our first two webcourses on this material in 2009 and 2010.

Thank you to the mentors, teachers and retreat guides in The Institute for Applied Meditation who have used The Map to Illumination for up to 20 years. Your experience has contributed valuable details and nuances to The Map: John Bassett, Alistair Beattie, Robin Carpenter, Bonnie Colby, Caroline Dale, Dilsha Happel, John Happel, Doug Johnson, Elijah Khan, John Kroeker, Dan McMannis, Jennifer Moore, Karen Poulson, Heather Redington, Linda Turner, Jeanie Underwood, Arjunada Vitos, and Catherine Warrick.

Preface

The Map-Makers

THERE IS A TERRITORY TO BE MAPPED.

Your heart begins beating at the quickening of your life, as soon as 18 days after conception; two billion or so beats later, the beating of your heart stops and ends your life, and in between, your heart beats out the steps of your life's journey. For some it's like a journey on horseback; for others, it's like a plane ride. Still others journey on foot. No matter how you travel or at what speed, you have to pass certain landmarks: valleys, mountains, bridges, dry deserts and lush regions. It is the same for all of us. We are all travelers on this path. Plumbers and priests, laborers and lawyers, nurses and newscasters—we all follow our hearts along the same path to the same goal, the fulfillment of the purpose of life: *illumination*. We each reach as far as we can in this one life, some with closed eyes and some with open; some are dragged along and some run ahead; some stop and set up hotels for other travelers; and some who go ahead leave trail markers for those who follow. This book gives The Map of the pathway, knowledge of which will make for a smoother journey and allow us to travel farther.

The notion of a map for human development flies against the popular philosophy of simply being present in the moment. When you're in your heart you have a tremendous appreciation for the beauty and wonder of this moment, and you also feel a pull toward a distant goal. Your heart has a desire, a passion that will lead you to become what you were meant to be, so that you can fulfill the purpose for your creation. As you listen to your heart you will discover the path that has been prepared for you, the same path that has been traveled by everyone who has followed their heart.

If you are desire-less, you can be still and motionless on life's path, enjoying the moment, content with it. But as soon as you touch your heart, you will be reminded of your mission in life to make that unique contribution that only you can make. If you meditate with your heart, you'll see that you're not just at this place at this time, but you're everywhere along the path all the time. You are still the one who set out on this journey and you are already the one who will arrive. Celebrate how far you have come, attend to the opportunities of this time, prepare the way to the goal ahead, and be the captain of your life. *The present moment can be as large as a lifetime* if you extend the scope of your awareness to the whole of your path.

Some say there is nothing to learn and nowhere to go, and that anyway you are different at every moment. But there is a continuity in the changing, dynamic person that you are. So to know yourself you must be conscious of all that you have ever been, of that which you still are, and of all that you can become, which is already emerging, throughout time. In expanded consciousness, your present moment expands to include your past and your future. Remembering what has gone before and anticipating what lies before you on the path of your self-unfoldment, it's absolutely truthful to include your potential future in your present self-conception, just as a tulip seed anticipates and identifies with its coming floral form. Self-knowledge, then, requires an understanding of not only what has happened to you, but also what *is* happening to you, and where this experience will take you. This is the function of The Map.

It is important to understand that The Map is pragmatic and experiential. It has been developed for practical use in guiding ourselves and others through the process that leads to spiritual maturity. It is not only descriptive, it is operative: it not only describes the steps of the path, it also contains instructions that enable a traveler to reach the next step.

The Map is different from psychological descriptions of adult life that show a person moving from youthful, enthusiastic initiative, through mid-life crisis, to aged contentment. Such descriptions of human development do not show how the process can be sped up or extended farther, or even if that is possible. We're not content to observe the process of aging; we want to consciously operate the process of transformation.

Most people don't need to know there is a path or where they are on The Map because, spiritually, most people are like villagers who have never been to a city. Unless you're a traveler, or you're concerned for some reason about people in other lands, you don't need to know much geography. But if you want to explore the inner world, The Map we offer here is as valuable as any map of the outer world. A map is a guide left by those who have explored the territory; it points out the popular spots, the dangerous areas, the main roads, the shortcuts and the milestones. When you have clarity about where you are and where you want to be, you can navigate through obstacles that otherwise might seem insurmountable and make your way with greater confidence.

This book will help you understand where you have been on The Map and where you are likely to go next. You will see where you got stuck or lost your way, and where you have have made great progress. By doing so, you will have a more smooth, joyous journey. In the next chapters, you will be guided through The Map with a series of instructions and meditations to integrate your past experiences, current states and heart's desires into a life lived with stronger intention and purpose.

The Origin of The Map

Child development has been well understood and mapped from stage-to-stage—it is clear, for example, that an infant will walk before he or she can talk—and likewise the stages of adult development through physical and emotional maturity have recently been mapped by psychologists. But long ago the stages of life from individuation to spiritual maturity were mapped by the mystics, those masters of the inner world who sense and operate the oneness of reality. All the maps they have left us cover the same territory: the stepwise progression of experience-based wisdom and the corresponding creation of exemplary character.

The Map as presented here is sourced in the teachings of Hazrat Inayat Khan, based on his book, *Volume 10, The Path of Initiation.*[1] The path he describes was described and further developed by his son and our teacher, Pir Vilayat Inayat Khan (d. 2004), who taught us how to recognize the steps in our students.[2] We calibrated ourselves to his assessments of hundreds of students over three decades. The Map has been a topic of our contemplation since 1971 and we use The Map with our students and ourselves to anticipate and track progress on the Path of the Heart.

In any process of human transformation, there must be a map that makes sense of the series of changes that people go through. Every tradition has had its concept of the journey.

- The Native Americans described self development as a literal journey through the seen and unseen worlds.
- The ancient Egyptians described an alchemical transformation through six stages.
- Labyrinths express the journey as a series of turns.
- In the 13th century the 11-ring labyrinth was built into the floor of the Christian Chartres Cathedral in Paris.[3]
- Christian contemplatives such as Clement of Alexandria described the three large stages of the journey as *Katharsis* (purification), *Theoria* (Illumination), and *Theosis* (Union).[4]

---

[1] Khan, I. (1960-1964).

[2] See Khan, V. (1974), (1978), (1982), (1983), (1988), (1992), (1994), (1996), (2000), (2003)

[3] The labyrinth's description of the nine steps of the path is the subject of Chapter 5.

[4] Osborn (2008)

- The Eastern Orthodox described three categories of prayer: mental prayer, prayer with mind and heart, and unceasing prayer.[5]
- Abu Nasr al-Sarraj (d. 988) described "Seven Stations," which span steps one through nine.[6]
- The mystic-poets of the East and West have added texture and color to the map, especially Jelal-ud-Din Rumi and William Shakespeare.[7]
- The 12th century Chinese master Kakuan described the path as a relationship with an ox that must be found, tamed and ridden home.[8]
- Farid ud-Din Attar, who wrote *The Conference of the Birds* in the year 1177, described the first nine steps of the path in allegorical terms.[9]
- Twentieth-century researchers like Erik Erikson, Daniel Levinson and Clifford Anderson have described their research into adult psychological maturity, which is the first five steps of the path.[10]
- In the 1900's, Sufi teacher Hazrat Inayat Khan spoke extensively about The Map in 18 steps. It is this version, which incorporates all the previous maps and

---

[5] Kotsonis (2007), Logothetis (1982).

[6] See Al-Sarraj (2010).

[7] Barks (1995)

[8] The steps of the Chinese fable are compared to The Map in Appendix 1. See Reps (1998).

[9] Attar's allegory is compared to The Map in Appendix 2. See Attar (2003).

[10] Anderson (1995), Erikson (1994), Levinson (1986).

adds considerable detail, upon which we have based this book.

The Universality of The Map

The great mapmakers of the past all operated within some spiritual tradition, but their wisdom transcends their traditions. The experience of the heart is for everyone. All religions meet in the heart, which affords a direct encounter with the oneness of all beings and all things. Where the ordinary view sees people as separate from one another and from nature, students of the heart are grounded in the wholeness of all life, and comprehend deeply that this life is the embodiment of love. All share a common concern: how human beings can live better lives on this planet at this time, and how to give help to those who need it. Jelal-ud-Din Rumi, the 13th century founder of the Mevlana Order of Whirling Dervishes and the best-selling poet in the U. S. today, said, "I am neither Christian nor Jew, nor Hindu, nor Moslem. I am not of the East, nor of the West, nor of the Land, nor of the Sea... I have put duality away, as I have seen that the two worlds are one."[11]

In this work, we seek to integrate all realities—physical, emotional, and spiritual—to become co-creators of reality and accept the responsibility of incarnating the universe. It's serious business; only through love can we handle it.

We hope that The Map brings you new and profound insights into your spiritual journey and the nature of the spiritual path in general.

With love,
Puran and Susanna Bair

---

[11] Nicholson (1898, II)

Founders, The Institute for Applied Meditation

P.S. This book is a work in progress, and revisions are expected. For updates, please see the website for this book: *www.*followyourheart.*org*

Chapter 1
The Process of Becoming

THE GOAL OF HUMAN DEVELOPMENT is to manifest in one's body, mind, personality and behavior the pure qualities of Love, Harmony and Beauty, to explore the potentials of all being within one's own being, and to accomplish the purpose for which one was created. The path to this goal has been mapped by those who have traveled it before us. Your goal is not to become Christ or Quan Yin, or anyone who has inspired humanity in the past; their contribution has been made; your contribution is to be a fully realized version of yourself.

> With the maturity of your soul, you desire to probe the depths of life. You desire to discover the power latent within yourself, you long to know the source and goal of your life, you yearn to understand the aim and meaning of life, you wish to understand the inner significance of things, and you want to uncover all that is covered by form and name. You seek for insight into cause and effect, you want to touch the mystery of Time and Space,

and you wish to find the missing link between God and yourself—where you end, where God begins.[12]

How would you describe your spiritual goal, or to put it another way, the fulfillment of your life?

The time given for one human life is short, yet the list of our potentials is long. What would you like to become in your lifetime? How would you like to be remembered? The great personalities are known not only for what they accomplished but for the qualities of their hearts. It is the mystics who have left the strongest impressions upon the heart of humanity, with the result that they are adored and praised hundreds and thousands of years after their death.

The Great Turn

The goal of spiritual development has changed over the last five-thousand years, since the earliest spiritual texts, and this is appropriate as humanity has tried to answer the "Three Big Questions" of life, which we will discuss in the next chapter. The ancient Egyptians were fascinated with the *spiritual experience of death*: what happens to the soul after the body dies, what ethereal lands does it visit, what judgment does it endure, and what is its final destination? This experiential research passed into India and was continued by Yogis who invented meditation techniques that would take one as close to death as possible, while still being able to return and report on the experience. Buddhism developed a process to turn "the wheel of becoming" which rolls forward in life, backwards, to experience existence before life. This took the transcendent Yogi practice of *samadhi* to a further level, be-

[12] Hazrat Inayat Khan, Vol. 9, The Unity of Religious Ideals, Five Desires of Man, #4; this quote, along with others in this book, has been adjusted to meet modern gender norms.

yond even the concept of space, time and self.[13] Further development in this direction is not possible, so later mystics, starting with Christ, took mysticism in the opposite direction: *what is the spiritual experience of life*?

Thus the spiritual work made the great turn, a fundamental re-orientation in the goal of a spiritual life.

- A turn from the objective of becoming selfless and bodiless to becoming inclusive of spirit, ego, mind, and body.
- From becoming an angelic light to becoming a human lamp.
- Before the turn, a mystic might have said, "Become pure, luminous consciousness." After the turn, mystics said, "Embody your angelic inheritance, incorporate the heavenly energy into the fabric of your body, and demonstrate divine love in your personality."
- The early objective of Vedanta was to attain liberation (*moksha*), free from the illusion of the material world. The objective now is to become worthy of responsibility as a co-creator of the worlds: as above, so below.
- Instead of "Be here now,"[14] the new mantra is "Be everywhere always."[15]
- We are updating the "Doctrine of Impermanence,"[16] in which all creation is constantly changing and therefor

---

[13] See the *Yoga Sutras* of Patanjali, in Bryant (2009). For comments on Samadhi by a modern master, see Khan, V (1992), (2000).

[14] Ram Dass (1971)

[15] A frequent saying of Pir Vilayat Inayat Khan.

[16] Impermanence is one of the three essential doctrines of Buddhism. See *The Dhammapada,* in Carter (2008).

has no fixed essence, to incorporate the principle of resurrection, in which profound events in human time can alter a soul and through it, the soul of humanity, forever.

- Instead of aspiring to be nothing, we are now aspiring to be everything, as in the mystics declaration, "I am a part of all things and all things are a part of me."
- To pursue nothingness, the path of a monk is required. The pursuit of everything is a path in life, with a family, a job, responsibilities, a healthy body, social life, etc.
- Those who aspire to be pure spirit have no need for a personality; those who aspire to be complete honor the personality as proof of their spiritual realization. If spirituality can't make you a more understanding friend, a more loving partner, a more powerful contributor, a more successful innovator, a more peaceful refuge, and a more inspiring resource, then you don't need it.

The new spiritual objectives that came after The Great Turn are mapped here in nine steps of adult development that trace the path from the earliest stage of individual formation to the goal of universal, spiritual realization, called "Illumination." The detailed descriptions of the steps show that The Great Turn did indeed develop the path further; liberation comes at Step Seven, and is then followed by a re-emergence of Self in Step Nine.

Along this path, one's individuality is (1) valued, tested, and affirmed, then (2) softened in relation to others while strengthened by extraordinary courage, and finally (3) superseded by an impersonal identity that is simultaneously within one's self and larger than self.

The first two stages are concerned with the development of the self, building the power to accomplish what one desires. The very end of the second stage dismantles the boundaries of self that one has constructed, which have become confining barriers to further growth and connectedness. Then the third stage develops a new sense of a boundary-less self where one's self-interest is no different than the interest of others or the need of Life itself.

There is a further Stage Four which is a dedication to the service of the hearts of others and the Heart of All. This step is beyond the goal of personal fulfillment; although human development is never-ending, the intention in Stage Four is only to be of service. If any personal growth occurs as well, it will be used for greater service.

By helping us to understand the path that every soul is treading in life, The Map can help us focus on the lessons of this moment instead of repeating the lessons of the past or attempting a work for which we are not yet ready. Every step of this path is exalted, and each step gives the preparation we need for the next step.

Some of the steps are difficult while others are easy; some steps seem undesirable, others are glorious; to some steps we aspire and to other steps we surrender, yet both positive and negative experiences are important to push us forward. The Map shows that the odd-numbered steps are steps in glory, alternating with even-numbered steps in surrender.

Without the Map, we might think that the path should be all uphill, and that downhill sections are due to our errors. The Map tells us that growth and learning are the objectives of life, not happiness or constancy. There may be periods when we feel happy and stable, but the nature of the universe is dynamic, so change is inevitable. We learn to take all that is given as our path in life, and to give to our path of growth all the life we have.

Therefor, there is as much value in the down cycles as in the up cycles. It is folly to try to sustain positivity; this deprives us of the opportunity to appreciate the insights, emotions, energy and full experience of all that life offers us. Inevitably, with a movement like that of ocean waves, positive will follow negative, which will turn into positive. But our assessment of positive and negative simply reflects our expectations. What seemed positive might later seem negative, and vice-versa, so eventually one stops evaluating life by such personal judgments and sees the positive in the negative and the negative in the positive. This is the beginning of a life in harmony. The way to arrive at that harmony is to appreciate all, including disappointment, loss, failure and illness, all as part of the preparation needed to fulfill the purpose of your life.

Whatever your purpose is, it will certainly involve some form of service. In the beginning steps, perhaps the aim of service to others is not so clear, or if there is a desire to help others, the type of service is unclear. First you have to master your mind through concentration, to develop the power to accomplish what you want to accomplish. Then, the opening of your heart sensitizes you to your deep longings and to the needs of others. You discover that you are willing to sacrifice to pursue a passionate desire: your art changes from self-expression to helping others see; your politics changes from self-interest to the common good; your relationships change from receiving to giving; your work becomes inspired by your passion. Further advancement on the path will take you to greater levels of service.

The Map also tells us that progress is about taking responsibility. The trinity of Creator, creation and created becomes one in a state of unity; the created become creative creators, co-responsible for creation. This responsibility is not borne alone; it is shared with all those who also feel responsible for an area of interest, a group of people, or a geographic area. Our work individually is to learn and practice the ability to move energy, which lifts or sinks consciousness like a tide carries a boat, so that we can become effective and responsible for all within our sphere of influence.

Thus, the Map reveals a path of tremendous importance not only to ourselves, but to the development of the world towards its goal of reflecting on earth the qualities of heaven. That is the purpose we are assigned collectively, and for that purpose we are drawn to follow our hearts, which hold the memory the of heavenly states we seek to embody. The more we know about it, the better. Each of us, within our sphere of influence and to the extent of our attunement, has a role to play in the awakening of humankind.

Chapter 2
The Three Big Questions

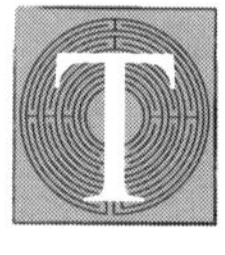HERE ARE THREE BIG QUESTIONS IN LIFE:

1. Who am I?
2. Who is God?
3. What is our relationship?

Your answers to these questions define your spiritual realization and determine your attitude toward your body, your personality, the quality of your relationships, your sense of purpose in life, and generally, your behavior in any situation. This realization changes as it evolves and passes through the stages of the spiritual path. Each stage of the path reduces fear, misery and doubt and brings new and greater challenges.

How do you answer the Three Big Questions?

Your answers to the three big questions will progress along four basic stages, as follows.

1. **Separate Beings.** "I am an individual, separate from other individuals, and God, if there is such a thing, is

something separate from me. My wishes that I express to the universe are generally not fulfilled. Good and bad things happen to me regardless of my intention. My responsibility toward the universe is not at all clear."

2. **Connected Beings.** "I am an individual in a network of interconnected people whose thoughts, words and actions affect each other through linkages between our hearts. All that I send out from my heart echoes in the Universal Being in which we all exist and returns to me."

3. **One Being.** "My individual self and the Universal Being are the extremes of a spectrum that I call myself. Sometimes I function on the individual end of the spectrum as any one does, but I am aware of an infinite spirit within myself and I can dissolve my identity in the sea of that wholeness. I realize the spirit within myself is the same spirit within every person; consequently, I feel every person as myself, and the feelings of every person in myself."

4. **An Instrument in Service to All.** "I realize myself as an instrument of the Universal Being: my body is an outgrowth of the body of the planet; my mind picks up the thinking of the universe; my emotions reproduce the cosmic emotions of the spinning planets and atoms; my soul is a ray of the Source of Light. Consequently, I feel a responsibility as an instrument of the Universal Being to carry out the universe's intention."

The answer of each stage corresponds to the discovery of a deeper and more essential aspect of self.

- Separation is the experience of your mind.
- Connectedness is the experience of your heart.
- Oneness is the experience of your spirit.

- Service is the experience of yourself as an instrument of spirit.

Let's explore each of these four discoveries, shown graphically in Figure 1.

Stage One: Mind

The first stage, of separate individuality, is the understanding of the mind without heart. The mind is basically a faculty for recognizing patterns. It observes cause and effect, discriminating between faces and voices to identify one person out of many; the mind plans and reasons. The great skill of the mind in discerning difference gives the mind-centered person the experience: "you are different from me." Because of this difference and separation, one can reasonably expect that this statement is not too far behind: "I can take advantage of you without any disadvantage to me."

From what appears to the senses, your mind creates a concept of the world in which other people exist outside of yourself, and that invisible forces occur beyond your control or intention. Consequently, when you operate in this stage of realization, you will worry about what might happen, you

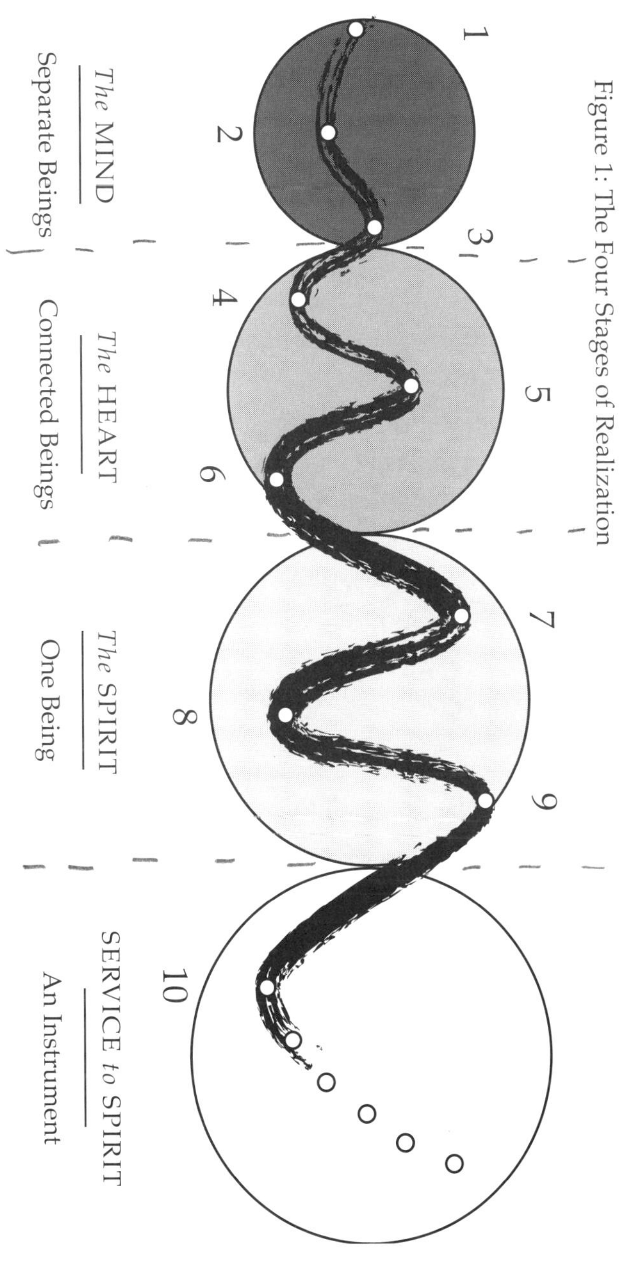

Figure 1: The Four Stages of Realization

will complain about what is happening, and you will doubt that the favorable things that did happen have any significance.

Most people spend most or all of their lives in Stage One, ignorant of what gives them true happiness, afraid of being overpowered, generally pessimistic, self-centered without knowing the self, intolerant of differences, critical of everyone, and isolated by an inability to understand and sympathize with others.

There is no fault in this and no blame; the world as perceived by the mind is a hostile and confusing place where people compete for diminishing resources to accomplish mutually-exclusive goals. The best that can be expected of people who see others as external and separate from themselves, is the principle of reciprocity: I will do such-and-such for you and I expect you will do the same for me. This behavior is similar to commercial transactions; while each transaction may be fair, by your own mental assessment of what you give and what you'll get, there is no generosity or graciousness in a kind of black-and-white world.[17]

There are three steps in the development of the mind, and when the third step is realized, the result is good boundaries between yourself and others, competency in work, and harmony and trust in relationships. These three steps can be a long process, as they build concentration, persistence, objectivity and knowledge. Persons with a well-developed mind are confident in their opinions, dependable

[17] The Golden Rule is: *Do unto others as you would have them do unto you*. This shows the attempt of the prophets to meet the average person where they are, in the Stage of the mind.

in their duty, predictable, reliable, content, and reasonable.

Stage Two: Heart

When you feel connected to others, it shows the opening of your heart, that deeper aspect of yourself that is shared, like the collective unconscious, and which reflects like a mirror the outer world upon your inner world and the inner upon the outer.[18] The faculty of heart is a deeper faculty than the mind; the world of feeling is infinitely richer than the world of appearance. The opening of your heart is an emotional and spiritual experience that allows you to see in the present moment the beauty and wonder in any person or situation, and to see into the future the potential that is not yet developed.

Your heart reveals a world of beauty, wisdom and fulfillment that makes everything one has accomplished and understood before seem insignificant. Everyone has had glimpses of this world, but most people revert back to reliance on their rational mind to decide what is real and what is not. But the mind is not qualified to judge the world of the heart, for the mind cannot perceive the invisible yet powerful reality which is the heart's domain.

The second stage, the stage of heart, gives you your ideals, optimism and creativity. Your heart powers an extraordinary level of success as it points to the real purpose of your life. You learn how to surrender to love willingly and resist falsehood heroically. Depression, poor self-image, addictions and resentments vanish in the heart's courage, creativity and forgiveness. Life in the heart cannot be compared to life in the mind; it's an entirely different way of seeing,

---

[18] Jung (1981)

feeling, working and being.

The behavior of this stage is called 'beneficence': since you recognize that all that comes out of you rebounds and comes back to you, you give your respect and help to everyone, whether they deserve it, or appreciate it, or not.

Stage One thinking may poke through Stage Two, making you doubt that your altruism and optimism will work, and making you worry you will be taken advantage of or ridiculed, but that's just the limitations of the mind's understanding. As long as your heart is energized you can regain the courage, creativity and joy of your natural condition.

Stage Three: Spirit

The third stage is seldom attained. The conviction that we are all united in a comprehensive oneness comes when you can experience yourself as spirit.

- There are many different streams of thought and everyone has their own memories, so from the mind's point-of-view, it makes sense to think of people as separate and independent of each other.
- We are touched emotionally by different things, but the emotions we reach are the same, so from the heart's point-of-view, it seems we are all separate but connected.
- Every soul is unique, but behind every soul there is one spirit that divides itself like rays of one light. When we perceive spirit, we perceive our unity with every being and form.

Therefor Stage Three comes from an awareness of your spirit, which you then realize is not your own; it is universal. This gives the direct, personal experience of the universe within yourself and yourself within the universe.

The third stage is the awakening that mystics have aspired to, experienced and taught to their disciples, called by various names like "unity," "enlightenment," "illumination," or "transfiguration," depending upon the tradition one follows. In this stage you discover and come to know that your individuality is but an appearance of the One and Only Being in a new and unique way.

In unity consciousness, both "I" and "you" are absorbed in the one Life that incorporates all, within and without, beneath and beyond. This one, all-encompassing Life is spoken of in the Bible verse, "In God we live, and move, and have our being."

It is love that leads you to this stage—not love for a person, but the longing your heart has to be immersed in Love itself, unlimited and unconditional. This divine Love will be expressed as love for others, and received from the hearts of others, and it will be felt always as the essential nature of your heart.

Stage Four: Service to Spirit

In Stage Three, individuality is immersed in a union with All, like a drop of water in the ocean. In Stage Four, the All directs the individual according to Its purpose, like the ocean rising up in a wave. You may pursue a career, you may have a love relationship, you may teach or you might heal others, but through whatever you do, you are conscious that your life is being directed and assimilated by the One who is Life itself.

In Stage Four, you are not using your heart to reveal hidden beauty, solve problems and advance your relationships and work, as you did in stage two. Neither are you absorbed into the Universal Being as in Stage Three. Instead, you are asking the universe to speak through your heart to direct your life, with complete trust in, and dedication to, the guidance of your heart. You are not using your heart; The Heart is using you. In this stage, there is no more conflict between the individual will and the divine will, for the divine will appears in your heart as your own wish.

There is also a fifth and final stage, but the description of that is reserved for those who are knocking on its gate.

Chapter 3
Realization

HAT IS REALIZATION?

To what shall you attribute the circumstances of your life—are they due to your childhood, luck, hard work, accidents of good or bad health, the actions of people upon you, the reactions of your actions upon others, impersonal forces of nature, the Grace of God? The view of the mystics is that the challenges you have, all that you're thankful for, and all that you pursue are due to the lens through which you see the world, called your *realization*. As your realization progresses, the scope of your life expands, giving you access to further dimensions of insight, energy, purpose and opportunity.

Your answers to the Three Big Questions of the last chapter are examples of realizations. Your realization is developed over time as your understanding of life: who you are, how people respond to you, what power you have to change things, what you cannot control. Your realization is a distillation of all your life's experience so far; it cannot be taught directly, nor does it result from a single event.

If you've built your own house, for example, you've learned a great deal about construction, plumbing and wiring. But the experience might have also helped you realize something about yourself and the world, for instance that you can implement some of what you imagine but not all, or that your creativity is inspired by physical objects that then lead you to imagine new forms and structures.

As this example shows, realization is something that you learn that is not restricted to particular places, times or people. A realization is a distillation of a large amount of experience to a simple truth that becomes embedded in your psyche to influence future behavior.

Any realization you gain, immediately becomes a part of the realization of humanity. That doesn't happen with facts you learn, or skills you develop, but a realization broadcasts across the species as it occurs. Because it is a personal discovery of an impersonal truth, every realization is a needed contribution to humanity's understanding and evolution.

It's difficult to notice your own realization because it's so close; it's fundamental to the way you work, relate, respond, and think about yourself and the world. Your realization is what you know beyond reason, that cannot be argued, and is the basis for your belief system and behavior. What you have realized is an assumption so deeply held that it's difficult to discern.

Consider: what do you know beyond a doubt, that you can not question, which you act upon automatically?

- One person might know that his accomplishments are largely driven by luck. Failure has taught him that there are uncontrollable forces which determine his success.

- Another might know that she can achieve anything she sets her mind to, as long as she makes it her first priority and works at it tirelessly.
- One person may realize that, "People are basically trustworthy. Everyone is worthy of my respect."
- Another has realized, "Everyone is inherently selfish."
- When life seems overwhelming, one woman we know falls back to what she has realized and says, "It will always work out," expressing an unshakable optimism and faith.
- Another person in the same situation may fall into, "You have to watch out for yourself because no one else will." This is true, but so is the realization above.
- Countries and organizations have realizations too, that define themselves and determine the scope of their influence and contributions.

We can identify nine steps of realization to the goal of personal completeness, where each step incorporates the previous steps progressively. You get to the third step, for example, by completing steps one and two.

Examples of Realization

Richard is a single man driven to success in business and finding a wife. His attempts at relationships have been hampered by his inability to trust someone. One could say that his problem is due to an overly critical mother, a poor parental model of adult relationships, a series of disappointing early friendships, a trauma that has made him insecure in his ability to love and be loved, a damaged first chakra, or many other causes.

All of these potential causes are in the past; the present result from his life's experience so far is his realization. The past can't be changed, but the realization he has created from all his experience is in the present, and this *can* be changed. This is a book about realization: what it is, its sequential steps, the assessment of your step of realization, and how to attain the next step.

In terms of The Map, Richard is in Step One, able to make a tentative commitment, but suspicious of relationships. Progress in being able to trust will not likely come from the love relationship he is trying to form, but from an advance in realization caused by inner discoveries about himself and his own trustworthiness, probably aided by a teacher or mentor who is eminently trustworthy. Richard's realization will affect every relationship he has, with lovers, bosses, co-workers, family and friends. When his realization develops to the third step, he will find it easy to be trusting, supportive, harmonious, understanding relationships everywhere he goes.

Joan is a real-estate broker in a small town where she is well-known but not well-liked, for Joan has the peculiar ability to make friends easily but alienate people she's known for awhile. She has a superior attitude that makes you feel put-down even if she's inviting you for dinner. You will quickly feel she likes you, so you'll be crushed when she belittles you to someone else. You could say her behavior comes from her feeling of not belonging, since she's foreign-born, or the incest by her father, or her wealth. We would say those are all contributing causes among others that have created the fourth step in realization, which is Joan's ability to feel something great in a person, but betrayed when he or she can't sustain what Joan sees.

Karen is a full professor of economics at an eastern university who is well-respected and frequently published. Her career is star-studded with speaking engagements, political appointments, consulting and board positions, so it's surprising to hear her say, "I don't know anything about economics, and I don't think anyone else does either. All the 'principles' I thought were true are at best relative truths, so all I can ever say is, 'It depends.'" Instead of enjoying the fruits of the reputation she has built up, she has become unmotivated and cynical. Is it a mid-life crisis, chronic fatigue, depression? A mystic might say it is typical and necessary to proceed to this step of realization after great success, to prepare for the transition from relative truths to universal truth. This is Step Six of realization, an advanced stage following great success, when all achievements become unimportant, even embarrassing, for having given one the illusion of knowing something.

Realization is a measure of spiritual growth

Life is about growth and Life pushes all living beings to grow. There is growth possible at every level of our selves: physical growth, mental growth, emotional growth and spiritual growth. The measure of physical growth is height and weight; the measure of spiritual growth is realization. Just as your mind is curious and your heart longs for emotional connection, your soul desires to express itself and manifest its potential, which is also expanding.

The evidence of spiritual growth is seen in your demonstrable skill in directing your mind, heart and spirit, and that skill is only possible after you have realized the nature of your mind, heart and spirit. Taking a step in realization occurs first, then, after some time of integration, behavior develops to implement the realization. For example, to operate your heart in actual life situations requires an inner realization of of the presence and power of your heart. Even before a realization becomes actionable, it can be sensed by someone who knows the invisible signals of that step and has personally advanced several steps beyond that realization. (See the Chapters 22 and 23 for more on the signs of realization.)

Applied Realization

Realization begins with an inner experience, a feeling, a longing, a desire, a dimly-understood sense of things. It develops into a conviction and undeniable knowing. It is completed when it becomes actionable in your personality. For example, you might have a belief that all people are connected in a way that makes us feel what another feels, but then speak to someone in a hurtful way. The *realization* of connection is a further development of the *belief* in connection. When it becomes a realization, then you will notice that your words make you feel as bad as the person you hurt. A further development is to always and automatically act towards others in a way that makes you both feel great.

Manifesting your realization in behavior will strengthen and enrich your realization; your outer experience will affect your inner experience.

Realization is different from skill. All skills are obtained through some combination of native talent, practice, and coaching from a teacher. Attaining skill at something like music, basketball, or painting, can and often does lead to

Chapter 4
The Benefits of Each Step

THE MIND (STAGE 1) IS A CRITICAL instrument; it is built to discriminate differences, and this allows us to identify faces and voices and compare one thing to another. When this critic focuses on others, they appear to be strange and inferior or superior to our selves, thereby strengthening the sense of a separate and distinct self. When you apply this critic to yourself, your own flaws appear magnified. Your heart, however, is accepting and embracing of others and yourself (Stage 2).

The Mind, Step 1

The mind processes alternatives and makes decisions; the ability to act upon your own decision is the first step of individuality. Choosing among alternatives is making a commitment, and that is a powerful personal statement. Even if the decision turns out to have been wrong, the ability to commit to something or someone is a great advance. The initiative gives a sense of power that defeats helplessness and victimhood. If you can't commit to do what you want to realization, for example that beauty must be created, not found, and that persistence and concentration are necessary for success. But while a skillful basketball player must have realized the value of teamwork, perhaps he hasn't realized that his teammates, and his wife and children, are more helped by compliments than by complaints.

If a person has attained great levels of personal skill, but also shows selfishness, petulance, and disrespect for others, then low realization is indicated.

Your step of realization may be quite different in the different areas of your life. We look at four areas of life: (1) spirit, (2) relationships, (3) accomplishment, and (4) health. Your spiritual realization is always the highest of your realizations. But you could be world-renowned in your work, for example, and still not treat your spouse with respect. Or you could have developed close relationships but not accomplish your goals.

A principle of personal transformation is that advances in spiritual realization will spill over to realization in your relationships, in accomplishing goals, and in your health. Once you feel the power of your heart, for example, your career will take off with new-found creativity and courage.

do, then you are at the mercy of the decisions and initiatives of others. When you can commit, you take your destiny in your own hand.

The Mind, Step 2

The second step strengthens your commitment by testing it with adversity. With the first bump in the road we question whether we have gone the right way. As more bumps and difficulties come, you will either turn back, or find within yourself some conviction that overcomes the obstacles, gaining self-confidence. There are always obstacles to whatever action you take and they serve to strengthen your resolve and persistence.

The Mind, Step 3

When your decision is fully settled and no longer debated internally, your mind becomes calmer, and anxiety and worry diminish. The peaceful mind is a great companion.

But if your mind is not peaceful because your decisions and commitments are not settled, then you might have sleeplessness, worry, fear, confusion, and low self-esteem, as you continually debate your decision. A particularly difficult case of this is when you require another to prove that they love you. The testing can go on for years until you finally accept that you are loved, or not.

The attainment of Step 3 is a demonstration of concentrated focus, will-power, self-mastery, and contentment.

The Heart, Step 4

The opening of the heart is a dramatic and emotional experience of great joy and wonder. It is also unsettling because it opens a new, more wonderful world of rich emotion. It's the opening of your heart that gives you your idealism, and that can make you very dissatisfied with the way things are. But once you've seen the world in full-color, there's no going back to black-and-white.

At Step 4, all that you've accomplished in your life so far seems very little. There is a strong desire to change yourself completely, in keeping with the new vision you have of life. This is the beginning of a sense of purpose, that your life has a special meaning and you've been created and prepared to make a unique contribution. Some people sacrifice their job or their relationship to pursue something that appeals to their new awareness of expanded possibilities. Others gain a deeper appreciation for the people and circumstances of their life because they are awakened to the profound beauty and meaning they represent.

The Heart, Step 5

There is an emotional intelligence beyond the intelligence of the mind. In Step 5 this emotional intelligence is harnessed to creativity, giving you the ability to apply the power of your passion to the challenges of doing something great. The feeling of success and satisfaction of Step 3, which became the longing of Step 4, is now greater than ever. Your confidence has reached an extraordinary level and your expert reputation is deserved.

This step is demonstrated by accomplishing something that expresses your ideal. It is not just success in the eyes of the world, but it is success in that which you feel is a priority for the world. Your accomplishment has not been only an act of persistence, hard work and discipline; you have aimed for your ideal, and you've satisfied it.

The Heart, Step 6

The expertise of Step 5 is the pinnacle of individual power and development; there is no further evolution in that direction. Paradoxically, your greatness has become your greatest fault. What you have accomplished and all that you have excelled in has defined you and limited you to that definition. There is so much more of your potential to discover, yet it is covered by the part of yourself that has been so wonderfully developed. To go farther toward the fulfillment of your purpose and potential, you will have to unlearn what you have learned about personal power so you can discover the impersonal power available to you. If you are willing to surrender the self you have created you can discover, in the next step, the self who creates.

In many people there is a feeling for something beyond, a longing for the experience of infinity and eternity, for the unseen world and the spirit behind the outer forms. This step is the preparation for that experience which is so grand it cannot be contained within an individual identity. The universe can only be experienced by itself; to feel the universe you must identify with the universe. But are you willing to feel all that humanity feels? If you are only willing to feel part of reality, say the blissful part, then you will have the experience of bliss, not reality, and you will still be longing for the Presence of God (Stage 3).

The Spirit, Step 7

The benefit of Step 7 is that it overwhelms you with the experience you have always sought, even when you doubted it could be reached. The invisible world opens up to you and you see the Face of God: the inner Being of every being, the light of every soul, the beauty of the hidden, and the unconditional love that binds the whole of creation. This opening leaves you deeply satisfied, honored, humbled, overwhelmed and bewildered.

This is the peak experience of a lifetime if it occurs even once. But the mystic desires to make this experience repeatable and reliable. Initially, the experience of unity will be difficult to incorporate into the duality of life but, after many peak experiences, it becomes integrated into a binocular vision of reality: individuality and universality co-exist.

The Spirit, Step 8

Step 8 gives you infallible guidance upon which you come to rely completely. Your relationship with your heart has matured to the point that you trust it more than your mind. You are then able to leap to decisions that logic could not support. While that would seem dangerous to someone at an earlier step, at this point listening to your heart's guidance seems like the most accurate, dependable and practical way to live.

The eighth step develops into what the mystics call "Dependence on God," which now has a very tangible meaning: complete dependence on your heart to guide your decisions and power your choices. This dependence would not be possible if you could not reliably ask questions of, and receive answers from, your heart. When that two-way communication becomes reliable, then life in the heart becomes the only acceptable way to live.

The Spirit, Step 9

The experience of union is finally integrated into your personality. You still flip back-and-forth between a dualistic vision and a vision of unity, because this is necessary to function in life, but the experience of the presence of spirit is always with you: it breaks through your attention spontaneously, and you can recall it deliberately.

This place in the path is delightful, void of the stress, longing and aspiration that a seeker typically feels. It is your natural state, your home, that you have sought so long. Your personality is now complete and you have attained the goal of self-realization. There is no more blame of anyone for anything, no fear and no self-doubt. Your life is a blessing that you pass on freely without reservation. The depressions and anxieties of others are all familiar to you as your own, but you have become immune to their effects on you personally. You offer sympathy to everyone who suffers, which touches you deeply, but you do not despair for the same reasons they despair, nor are you joyful for the reasons they are joyful. Life is endlessly fascinating and every moment is a discovery of the One who appears in the multiplicity.

The Service to Spirit, Stage 4: Step 10 and beyond

Emerging from the contentment of Step Nine, you are empowered to take your part in the cosmic drama, as a significant contributor. The challenges you have at this stage are not your own; they appear as reflections within you of the struggles of humanity. You don't work alone, but in concert with others who feel the imperative of this time and the condition of the heart of humanity. Coordinating your efforts, you apply consciousness to operate subtle energies for effects that others would not notice or consider relevant to the urgencies of the moment. This may result in your working in an unusual way, mysterious to others.

As one mystic said, "If God had revealed to you what God has revealed to me, you would not be doing what you're doing. And furthermore, if God had not revealed to me what God has not revealed to you, I would not be doing what I am doing." (Al Hallaj, d. 922)[19]

[19] Massignon (1994)

Chapter 5

Mentoring at Each Step

TO GIVE AN EXAMPLE OF HOW THE STEPS of realization might affect your practical life, imagine that you are a mentor and you're asked to give advice to a client who comes to you complaining about something their friend said or did. Your advice should be appropriate to your client's station, the furthest step they have realized on the path. If you speak to a lower station, your client will be insulted or dismissive. If you speak beyond their station, your client may be inspired by it, but will still be unable to implement your advice. People cannot behave convincingly beyond their station, and it would be rude to expect it of them. But we can use the situation to teach the steps of heart development and help the client to practice a response that is perhaps one step further than they would usually respond.

Step 0

A client that has not yet taken the first step, of commitment, will be feeling, "I don't need people like that for friends. I will avoid him from now on." We would never encourage this way of thinking; this client needs help with honoring friendships.

Step 1

Once the client has made an explicit or implicit commitment to develop a friendship, we want to encourage that commitment. So you might say to the client, **"You said you wanted to be friends with her, so remember, her problem is not your problem, and see if you can maintain this relationship, for your own benefit"** In this stage of the mind, people see others as separate from themselves. With a client at this early stage of realization, all you have to work with is the benefit your client will receive herself from forming a friendship. At this step, you have to emphasize strong boundaries with a client to keep her focused on her own issues.

Step 2

The friend must test the friendship in order to strengthen it, so some disagreeable speech or action will certainly occur in the beginning, and even throughout, the relationship. For example, a person who is normally punctual will be late for a meeting, to test whether you are willing to wait for him. If you will wait, then he feels more secure in the relationship. If you're not willing to wait, then he knows that if some emergency arises you won't be someone he can depend upon. So you might advise, **"He is testing you; show him that the friendship is valuable to you by overlooking his behavior."** The client's mind can accept that testing is necessary to measure a relationship, and that he also tests his friend.

Step 3

If your client has withstood her friend's previous tests to

demonstrate mutual commitment to the relationship and ultimately bring them closer, then we could interpret the disagreeable event as not a test, but rather an expression of a need of the friend. For your client to reach the third step she must be able to consider the needs of her friends. Advise your client to be understanding: **"Consider what you would like your friend to do for you if you were the one who was upset."**

This reciprocity is the most you can expect from anyone who lives in their mind. It's the classic, Golden Rule: "Do unto others what you would have others do unto you." This advice is quite reasonable and fair, so most people can accept it. But if your client is in love, or has an open heart toward her friend, then she is likely to say to you, "Do you want me to treat my dear friend like a used-car salesman, always thinking about what's *fair*?" That client is ready for the advice of Step Four.

Step 4

When the heart has been struck, the advice must change from understanding, to sympathy and forgiveness. At this stage, every situation is an opportunity to exercise the heart. Advise your client to see with his heart: **"Remember all that you admire and respect in your friend. Do not burden his heart with criticism or blame; inspire him with praise."** For example, instead of criticizing his friend's tardiness, he could say, "I'm so looking forward to what you have to say; you always have such good insights." Learning to praise instead of blame is one of the great accomplishments in life, but it's only sincere at this step, when your heart can see the qualities of your friend's heart.

Step 5

The power of your heart has emerged at this step, providing enough energy to energize the hearts of others. Your client can now see her friend's behavior as simply a temporary weakness of heart, which everyone has from time-to-time. A person at this step stays focused on what she can contribute to the unfoldment of others and to unleash the potential of a team. This is not a "should," it's natural because she feels her heart is powerful and influential. Tell your client, **"You know how to energize and inspire others, now tell me what you can do to make this relationship work."**

Step 6

The heart at Step Six has become so sensitive and so familiar with the full range of human emotions that a person can empathize with anyone. Whatever his friend is going though, this client will be able to recognize and remember the same feeling in himself. For this client, you can advise, **"What is irritating about your friend is also irritating within yourself."**

This is often said, and one often nods in agreement, but it is seldom experienced. For the vast majority, this advice is an example of overreaching a client's realization, with the result that the client ignores the advice or feels guilty in his inability to make use of it. The client for whom this is appropriate advice not only offers to help his friend, perhaps in a way that is unnoticed, but does so with great sympathy and without any sense of superiority.

Step 7

When a client has the realization of one spirit, their personal life becomes part of the one Life. Everything she says to anyone is a conversation with the one spirit, whether seen as an energy field or as the One Being. While your client is having a relationship with her friend, the one spirit is having a relationship with itself, and spirit itself will learn from the experience it's having in this interaction. This is always the case, but it is only relevant when one has the realization of spirit; otherwise, it is best to keep the discussion personal.

To a client with this realization, you can remind her that her personal relationship with her friend has cosmic implications: **"The two of you are involved in a dance typical of your respective archetypes and realizations. Whatever solution you find personally will accrue to the knowledge of humanity and help to resolve such issues in the future between people of similar archetypes and realization."**

Step 8

The client at Step Eight can consciously interact with spirit to receive guidance about how spirit can unite him with his friend. You can advise, **"Meet together in silence and ask for your hearts to speak to spirit and for spirit to speak to you and guide you to reconciliation."**

This discussion is not telling the other person what you want; it is both people openly and sincerely asking for help from the Spirit of Guidance. When people don't have the realization for this, such a meeting degenerates into sanctimonious platitudes to support restated opinions, but for two people with the realization of spirit, it becomes a profound opportunity to dialogue with the Heart of All.

Step 9

A client at Step Nine realizes that a solution that works for the other person works for her as well. She feels, "There is no difference between what is in your best-interest from what is in my own best-interest. A solution that is truly good for you will benefit me just as much." With such a client, you only have to remind her: **"Your relationship with your friend is a proxy for your relationship with God."** If she holds any complaint toward anyone, for anything, that complaint would be toward spirit, toward God. The universe is presenting itself in every aspect of its creation. Your friend is a manifestation of God. **"Look for the magnificence of God in your friend, even when she is irritated."**

Step 10

A client at Step Ten is not likely to bring a complaint about his friend, but there are surely people who are critical of him, and this will weigh upon his heart. He will always try to resolve a dispute because he realizes that he represents spirit for others, and so their relationship with spirit will be reflected upon him.

For someone who thinks spirit is mysterious, he will be mysterious. For someone who thinks spirit is frightening, he will be frightening. For those who love spirit, he will be dear, but for those who fear spirit, he will be intimidating. Your advice to this client could be, **"Relate to your friend as the all-pervading, all-embracing spirit would relate to him."** By doing this, you will help your friend to build a balanced and mature relationship with spirit, through yourself as proxy.

What advice would you give yourself in dealing with a complaint about your own friend?

Chapter 6
Life as a Journey

Come, seek, for search is the foundation of fortune: every success depends upon focusing the heart. —Rumi

LIFE IS TRULY A JOURNEY, and this journey has milestones. If your life were a book, where would the chapters end and begin? If your life could be traced on a map, where would there be big changes in direction or crucial passages?

Your first attempt to divide your journey into segments or your story into chapters will probably depend on external events: you went to college, you graduated or left, got married, changed careers, had a child, moved across the country, left the relationship, and other events of this type.

But The Map does not track outer events; The Map identifies the inner changes in realization that have caused changes in attitude that have in turn caused changes in behavior that led to external events. It is the inner changes that have been most significant; the invisible changes in realization have preceded the visible changes in life's circumstances.

One milestone in your life might be at a peak of happiness, power and success, with a breakthrough vision of a new horizon. Another milestone might be at a low point of disappointment, loss and failure, or a period of inward reflection and surrender. Both kinds of milestones are important, and together they make a path, like taking one step with the left foot and another with the right foot. We say we are following a path, which is a land-based metaphor, but it's more like a trip across a sea, where rhythmic waves lift us up and pull us down again, all the while driving us toward the shore.

Waves of the path

We can diagram this journey as a series of waves, like in Figure 1 on page 25, or as a series of arcs, where upward arcs are victories and downward arcs are surrenders, as in Figure 2 (see page 65).

Metaphorically, the waves get higher and deeper as one progresses. This is shown in the labyrinth, in arcs that get progressively longer. In both of these images, while there are obvious ups and downs, there is also a continual progress, even if it's not so easy to see. In Figure 1, the waves are moving one toward the right; in Figure 2, the arcs lead one toward the center. (For more details on the labyrinth, see Chapter 8.)

When you consider your life in this way, you are likely to find those milestones which we all share. We didn't all go to college, or get married, or have children, yet we all went through a series of inner changes, as far as we have gone thus far. To map the journey of life, we can't depend on any of the external signs that are specific to an individual as landmarks. This would be like writing a guide to crossing the U. S. that says, "Turn right at Robinson's Market." What if a traveler takes a different route, or what if Robinson's Market is no longer there, or what if the traveler goes by plane? The milestones we want to mark are those that everyone passes along the way, and these are internal, not external changes.

When you reflect upon your life's journey so far, can you identify a part of your path that was tremendously uplifting, followed by another part that was deeply disappointing, that led to an even more joyful part?

Resistance on the Path

Each step has its rules and challenges designed to hold the traveler there, either by contentment with the familiar or fear of the unknown. To leave one stage in pursuit of the next requires courage, strength, and initiative.

The change from one stage to another is as dramatic as the difference between running on land and swimming in water. You may know how to run very well but that doesn't prepare you for your first experience of being in deep water, unable to touch the ground. So it is with a person who has developed intellect but has not yet developed heart: the way one makes decisions, relates to people, manages stress, appreciates beauty, all these things change from one stage to another. The way a person thinks, feels and acts is so completely different, it's as if they live in a different world.

Most people proceed on the path unconsciously, pulled along by the natural forces of growth. Physical maturity proceeds automatically, and your mind develops as your interests require concentration. Your heart develops naturally too, through love, and spiritual development proceeds inevitably, by the end of your life if not before. But the pace of your development can slow or even stop for years, perhaps decades. If you tread the path consciously, then progress can be very rapid and you can soon reach stages of inspiration, joy, fearlessness and peace that few people reach in a lifetime.

Amir Khusro, a 13th century poet, wrote, "Beware, O travelers, the path has many charms; robbers and thieves are all along this path."[20] The charms that hold us back are pleasures that we mistake for real happiness, comforts of laziness and delusion. Growth requires change, and change is uncomfortable. We lull ourselves to sleep by claiming we are already as complete as we can be, or there is no path, or progress is not possible. The robbers and thieves on the path are fear of the next step and all that causes our precious life energy to be wasted.

We have seen so many people open the door to the next stage and close it again out of fear their lives would be disrupted, something would be lost, or they wouldn't be able to relate to their old friends if they entered that new room. It is often the case too that people who would like to take another step in their life simply don't have the energy to do so; perhaps they have poor health, physically or emotionally, or addictions have robbed them of their will-power, or past relationships have weakened their trust. These robbers and thieves can be overcome by knowledge of the path together with a practice like Heart Rhythm Meditation that restores heart energy.

Growth is the prime desire and directive of the universe.

---

[20] Khusro (2008)

All of life inherits this desire to grow, explore, and actualize all potentials. Therefore, from growth comes all happiness, while resistance to growth causes all unhappiness. From this, we can see how important it is to understand the process of growth to spiritual maturity.

Just as is the case with any journey, we do not always proceed upward; we forge ahead and drop back. There is elation and there is despair. Some progressions are a breakdown; some are a breakthrough. The alternating rise and fall of the wave pushes us forward, and the downward slopes are as effective in creating forward movement as the upward slopes.

There is a natural tendency to want to jump from one success to another success, as if you could jump from the crest of one wave to the crest of the next wave without descending into the trough between them. The heart, however, values all emotions and all parts of the path. We draw the path as a series of waves with crests and valleys or as a labyrinth of turns because we know that a retreat makes a necessary preparation for the next advance. Our faith is tested by the descents and our self-confidence is affirmed in the ascents. Both parts of the path are necessary, unavoidable and invaluable learning processes.

You can change jobs, houses, or relationships, and really change nothing at all until an inner realization comes. That inner realization makes everything different, although all may look the same from the outside.

One of our students told us of his past commitment to sports and his intense training during that time. He wrote that two accidents then followed, ending his athletic career. We asked him to consider whether there was some kind of inner change that came before the accidents—something he could see more clearly in hindsight. Was he feeling that achievement in sports wasn't enough for him? Was some other wish budding in his heart? He spoke of friends who had only entered his life after he stopped his athletic training. Although we didn't want to force any particular interpretation of events, we wanted to remind him that outer changes—even such a dramatic change as a serious accident that causes injury—occur only after an inner change. This is even more likely if that inner change is not honored. Another participant who had once been an athlete had a similar experience: her athletic career was ended by an illness, but before the virus, a shift had happened in her inner life. Keep this in mind as you write about your own milestones.

After sitting in Heart Rhythm Meditation to engage your heart—the seat of your non-logical emotional intelligence—write the real story of your life, not the story you tell the public. Write without limiting yourself; just let it pour out. Once you have let your heart tell your story, go through it and look for the critical changes in direction, purpose, or understanding. Look at how few are the crossroads of decision and how long are the journeys between those crossroads. Be proud of every twist and turn; after all, your path has brought you to where you are now, and this is a wonderful place, which will lead to an even more wonderful place.

Chapter 7

The Greatest Statement

I *WILL* IS THE GREATEST THING YOU CAN ever say. Why? Because it establishes your individuality. To exercise your personal will is to oppose or complement the power of nature, as you decide. It is the pronouncement, followed by the demonstration in action, of the power granted to the created by the creator—the power to co-create creation.

"I will" is important to us in our understanding of The Map because it has four levels of meaning that correspond to the four large stages of adult development.

Stage 1: The Mind

To say "I will" is to commit to doing something actively, to improve your condition or circumstance. It is the determination to pull yourself together. In the early parts of this phase of development, we choose what we *will* do based on what we *want*. The most basic statement of personal determination is the statement of personal desire, "I want." We've been saying this since we learned how to speak. Two-year olds are famous for being able to express their demands in terms like “No!” and “Give me that!” It's a great step in maturity to turn "I want" into "I will," by taking on oneself the responsibility for fulfilling one's own wants. So “Give me a cookie,” becomes “I will get a cookie from the jar,” or even, “I will make my own cookies.”

This level of will is what is usually meant by *will-power*: a committed, willful, focused determination requiring discipline and concentration. Worldly success results when you learn to consciously direct and hold your mind on the object of your desire—the task of the first three steps. It begins with making a commitment based on what you want.

Stage 2: The Heart

A further stage of maturity is to take responsibility for what “should” happen. Now “I will” becomes a promise made to another, to society, or to yourself to do the right thing: to take action to help another, to serve the whole, or to behave in a noble manner. This stage occurs when the self-concept, the meaning of “I,” has expanded beyond the person so that the needs and wants of others are now incorporated into one's own. This expansion is a characteristic of a developed heart.

Because the heart is now driving the will, a great power has been added to the mental will-power. Concentration is hard work, but now we have passion, which can easily hold the mind still. The Sufis say:

> *You never have to remind the lover to think of the beloved, for the lover sees the beloved's face everywhere.*

Stage 3: The Spirit

The next stage in willfulness is to allow to happen what Life wants to happen, and to harmonize one's self with this as much as possible. This requires an expanded consciousness, beyond sensitivity to one's friends and surroundings, to a sense of the intention behind Life.

Why should there be an "I" in "I will"? Can "I" control the weather, or even what happens in my own home? I am content to be so privileged that Life speaks to me and informs me of Her desire and intention.

Yet will-power is needed in Stage 3 as well. You must remember to keep tuning into the One Being, to stay energized, to remember whose Life you are living. This takes determination and dedication to spiritual practice.

Stage 4: Service to Spirit

"I will" can become so expanded that it becomes coincident with the will of the universe. Now it is the Whole Being Who says "I will" through its instrument: the enlightened individual. This is not the passive statement, "Let Thy will be done," as the Christian Lord's Prayer is commonly mistranslated. The Zoroastrian prayer from the Zendavestas expresses this fourth stage:

Let me be an instrument for the transfiguration of the world.

The same type of will was expressed by St. Francis in his prayer:

Lord, make me an instrument of Thy Peace.

In Stage Four your self is an instrument of the divine will, directed through guidance that emerges from within. God's will and your own will are not in conflict, nor could they ever be, as God's will operates through you to emerge as your own. The self re-emerges as an expression of the will of the universe.

Your Vision of Yourself

The expansion of the will in four stages corresponds to an expansion of your vision of your self that occurs in four stages as the path is progressed.

1. From the mind's point-of-view, the self is observed from a distance, and with considerable suspicion. It is very much like sailing on the surface of a lake, unaware of what swims beneath and hopeful that whatever is in the depth stays there. Sailors can become quite skilled in navigating the two-dimensional surface of the water but if the objective is to explore the lake, most of its volume goes unknown. There are sailors who don't know even how to swim!

   The depth of the lake can't actually be ignored. You can live without conscious awareness of your heart but not well, and not forever. There is a current in the lake that creates powerful waves on the surface, and even whirlpools. As much as the sailor might like to ignore the forces of the deep, and contend only with the wind (the forces of the world), the power of your heart in its depth is a mystery that draws all to itself.

   The metaphor breaks down here because the heart, unlike the lake, has a direct effect on the weather, the sailor and the boat. We might ignore our heart, but we cannot help but live within it, for it incorporates everyone and everything that we love.

   A mind-centered vision of yourself has clear boundaries of what is me and what is not me, similar to the discrimination your immune system must make between cells that are native and cells that are foreign invaders. However, your immune system has trouble making this distinction—bacteria slip by, giving illness, and cancer cells which are native but distorted, are not rejected—and so does your mind, because the distinction between self and others is an artificial concept, not a reality.

2. When your heart opens, your vision of yourself changes dramatically. Your vision of everything is different through the eyes of the heart. Since your heart reflects your soul, your heart is the portal through which you can experience your essential, real self. Until the heart is open, one cannot have a conscious experience of the Self, so one cannot know one's qualities or purpose in life.

   Now, with heart-centered consciousness, you can experience the wonder and the glory of life within and without. You can see your self reflected in the forms and beings around you, and you can feel how your heart attracts and shapes them. The boundaries of the self are thus blurred and self and others are no longer separate. Your normal experience is to feel deeply connected to others, and at some times you can feel more than connection—an intermingling of being itself. Thus, your notion of self is expanded in two ways: (1) toward the infinite, perfect, eternal aspect of your essential self, your soul, and (2) into a commingling of self with other selves. The impact of this expansion is profound for the human psyche, and brings a great happiness, success, and ultimately confusion.

3. The notion of self is expanded again to incorporate the impersonal, all-pervading, omnipresent spirit, the basis for the unity of all being. There is, it now seems to you,

one Actor on the stage of life, who plays all the roles. That is, the universe is discovering itself in us through our discoveries of the infinite in ourselves. We inherit the cosmic passion for self-completion by which the Whole Being completes itself.

4. But we are not mere observers of the cosmic symphony; we are featured soloists. Each one of us in the orchestra has a unique instrument that is needed by the divine Composer and Conductor to create the music they intend. The vibration we create together is the Music of the Spheres, but it is also my own music, what I myself choose to play when I am absorbed in the celestial song.

This step-wise development of the self-concept is truly an expansion where the earlier stages are incorporated in the later stages. It supersedes the compartmental concept of self where one is divided up into separate entities like mind and heart. What we mean by "heart" includes the mind as its surface: the mind is the surface of the heart. And our experience of the divine is that it includes the person; there is no "other."

The Development of Love

The same expansion occurs in love:

1. In the first stage there is love, but that love is self-centered and practical; it is thinking about love rather than being in love. This love means as much as "I love the effect you have on me," or "I love who I am when I'm with you," or as Jack Nicholson says in the movie *As Good As It Gets*, "You make me want to be a better man."

2. Hazrat Inayat Khan says, *It is love that makes one say, 'Thou, not I.'* Love exchanged between two loving hearts overwhelms the thought of self. There is no more score-

keeping, nor any expectation of returns. You love without reason, helpless to do otherwise.

3. In the stage of Spirit, you realize, "It is the Heart of All Being, the Universal Heart, that I love in every heart." The Beloved is your Self; there are not two, only One. And that One appears in every one, differently yet ever the same.
4. At the stage of realizing yourself to be an instrument of spirit, it is you who extends the divine love through your heart to others. Spirit loves those whom you love through you.

The Map to Illumination distinguishes four great stages: Mind, Heart, Spirit, and Service to Spirit. At this point, it will be easier to say which of these stages you are in then to say which step you are in, but the step will become clear as we add detail to the Map.

Chapter 8
The Labyrinth

THE FIRST THREE STAGES OF THE MAP, divided into nine steps, can be further understood by the use of the labyrinth. Figure 2 depicts the medieval design on the floor of Chartres Cathedral in France. It is a classic, 11-ring labyrinth, which contains an encoded form of the path to spiritual maturity. Note that a labyrinth is not a maze; everyone who enters the labyrinth at the bottom will eventually reach the center if they keep going. There are no blind alleys or wrong choices.

Try to imagine the experience of walking through the labyrinth as you can trace it with your finger, starting at the bottom of the labyrinth, moving from one number to the next. In this figure, the numbers indicate where each step ends, and the distance beyond that is the beginning of the next step. You immediately notice the twists and turns, and the fact that you are at times making rapid progress toward the center, your goal, and at other times, you are headed away from the center. You draw near, and then go far away, like waves rising and falling. Notice that the size of the rising and falling swings increases as you travel through the labyrinth. Experience the emotion of it; it's really a wonderful metaphor for life!

Figure 2: The Map and the Labyrinth

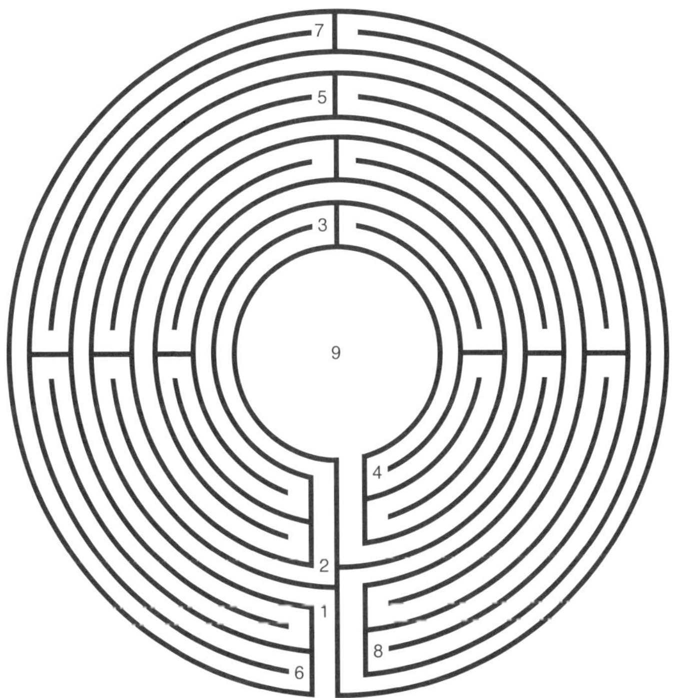

In order to understand how the labyrinth relates to The Map, we've placed the numbers of the nine steps on the labyrinth. The labyrinth has been in use for thousands of years, far predating the Chartres Cathedral, but its meaning as a description of the spiritual path has been kept hidden, passed from teacher to disciple. This is the first time, to our knowledge, that the steps of the path in the labyrinth have been published publicly.

The labyrinth correlates to the simpler wave model that we showed in Chapter 3, page 25, but reveals considerably more detail about the path from each step to the next. The wave model showed that the odd-numbered steps are upward, indicating celebration and ultimately glorification, while the even-numbered steps are downward, indicating a yielding in willing surrender. The combination creates a movement that pushes one forward along the path.

Figure 3: The Mind and the Heart in the Labyrinth

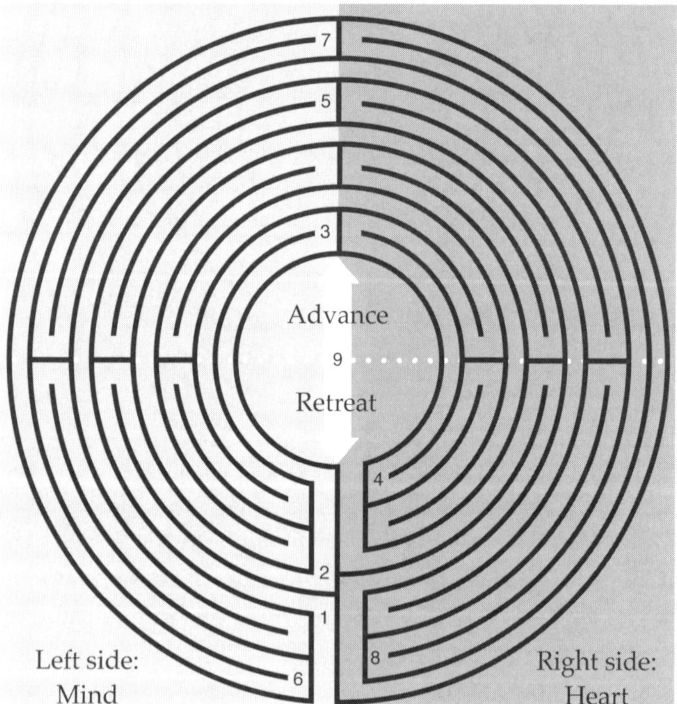

In the labyrinth, upward movements are advances, while downward movements are retreats, so the even steps of surrender are below the midpoint while the odd steps of glorification are above midpoint, except for the beginning and end steps (see Figure 3). The left side represents the mind, the right side, the heart. The labyrinth's depiction of the path is very useful in describing the twists and turns of the process of spiritual maturity. If you understand the importance of the turns of the path, the maze becomes a road map that can take you on a journey—in this one lifetime—to the place of personal and divine integration.

Step 1

Reaching the first station is easy; the path is straight and upward, until you hit a wall. This section of the path represents commitment—you boldly enter the labyrinth and your initiative gives you entry, for a short way.

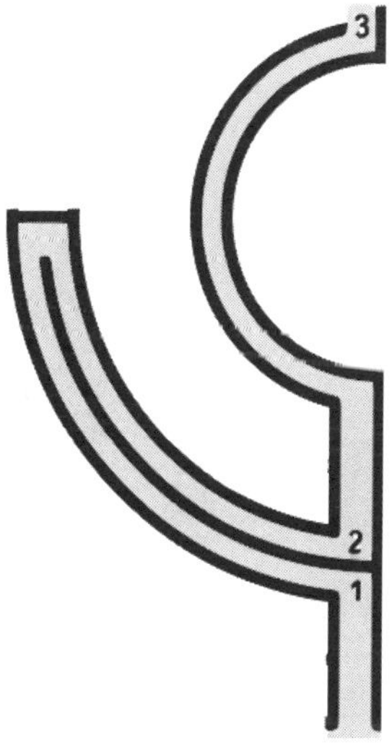

Step 2

The second station requires a test—will you turn the corner, and then accept a reversal in surrender that brings you back to nearly the same point as the first station? What has been gained by this loop? You've faced your first difficulty and demonstrated your determination.

Step 3

The third station is close to the goal in the center; it can seem that the goal has been reached. This gives confidence and self-assuredness. So far, the whole path has been on the left side, representing the mind. Mostly it has been an advancing, upward path, except for the reversal in Step 2. This section of the labyrinth is not difficult, which is why most people attain Step Three in their lifetime.

Step 4

From Step Three, the path moves away from the goal, to end up tantalizingly close to it again. You've become dissatisfied with the mental processes that have worked so well, until now. The path starts downward, indicating surrender, on the left, the mental side, then a short rise followed by a descent even lower than before to the bottom of this section of the path. This is the moment of disgust with the understanding of your mind. From the bottom, there is an ascent on the left: there is hope of a new way of seeing that can reveal what you haven't seen but you feel sure it is there. Then there is disappointment: this new vision is not going to come through the familiar mental capacity.

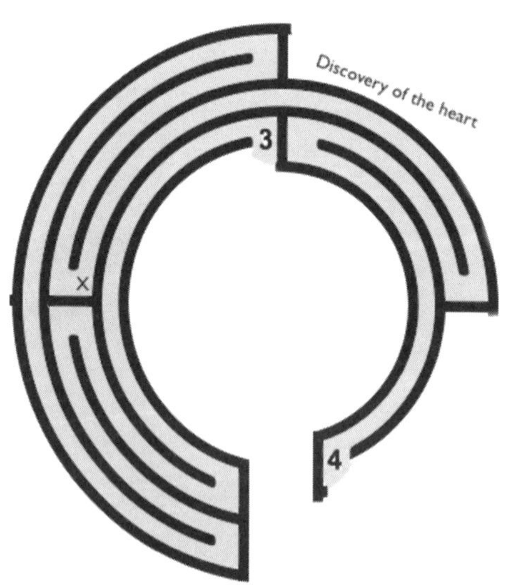

From the point marked "X", a breakthrough begins, leading to the first encounter with the heart, going from the mind's side, the left side, to enter the right side of the labyrinth for the first time. The heart's way of "seeing" reveals the perfect, eternal and infinite inherent in all things and beings. The heart sees love, harmony and beauty. You bow to this ideal, then bow again in surrender to your heart at Step Four.

The fourth step has brought you close to the goal, as the third step did, but now on the right side. This means the goal is now felt and adored, with the heart. A new way of relating to the world and to yourself has opened up with the opening of the heart.

Step 5

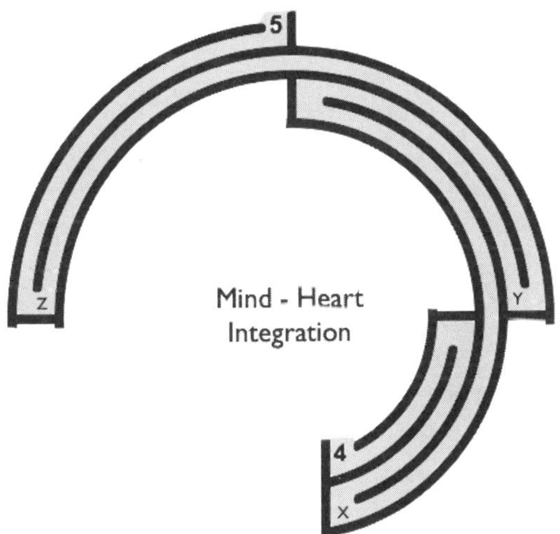

The fifth step is a great victory, requiring both the heart and the mind. It takes you to the second-most high position in the labyrinth. The long path through the heart (right side) shows how essential the heart is to achieving success. The mind is also needed, but now mind is inspired by heart.

From the beginning of Step Four, there is an exhilarating advance as you test the power of your heart, which is not yet complete. From the point marked "X", you make a great advance from the bottom of this section of the path upward as you learn how to use your heart's power in relationships and accomplishments. But at this step, you have not yet learned to trust the heart exclusively, so there will inevitably be a setback, to point "Y", when some conflict arises between the heart and mind. In the previous steps, heart-mind conflicts were always resolved in favor of the mind. But now that the joy, courage and creativity of the heart has been tapped, a new solution must be found, respecting both mind and heart. The sweep from point "Y" to point "Z" is a journey back to the mind, to balance and integrate the mind and heart. Your mind must bow to your heart, at point "Z", and then the integration is achieved at Step Five, balanced between the left and right sides, the mind and the heart, near the top of the labyrinth.

This is a time of great success in life, achieving even more than you had ever hoped—not just success, but success at something very important to yourself and very meaningful to society, something that could only be accomplished by the passion, creativity and courage of the heart.

Step 6

Step Six is a great surrender, called "the dark night." But the surrender is all in the mind—the surrender of the mind to the heart. It takes one back very close to the starting point of the labyrinth with the feeling, "I have come to know that I know nothing."

This section of the path is all in the mind, on the left side of the labyrinth. After the integration of mind and heart in Step Five, which may persist for a period of decades if it is reached at all, there eventually comes a discontent with the partnership. The heart, after all, has a much greater capacity for dealing with the struggles of life than the rational faculty of the mind, which also tires with age. If you cannot come to recognize that everything in life is better from the heart, and the best things in life are all about the heart, then you become a cynic. The fortunate ones who progress to Step Six are happy to declare, "My heart is a treasure my mind will never fathom."

Step 7

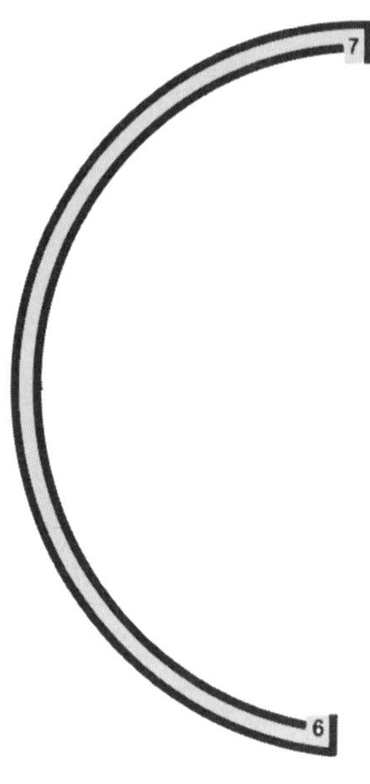

The hard work has been done; Step Seven is a sudden awakening in consciousness that takes one in a single sweep from the depth of unknowing to the supreme height of human experience: union with The All. Notice how simple this step is, once the heart has been prepared in Step Six. While many consider this enlightenment to be the spiritual zenith, our goal is still farther: the union of all, human and divine, heart and mind, integrated in the center of the labyrinth.

This step is done passively—that is, you attract this state rather than producing it. The next steps will bring you out of passivity into an active, bidirectional dialogue with the universe.

Step 8

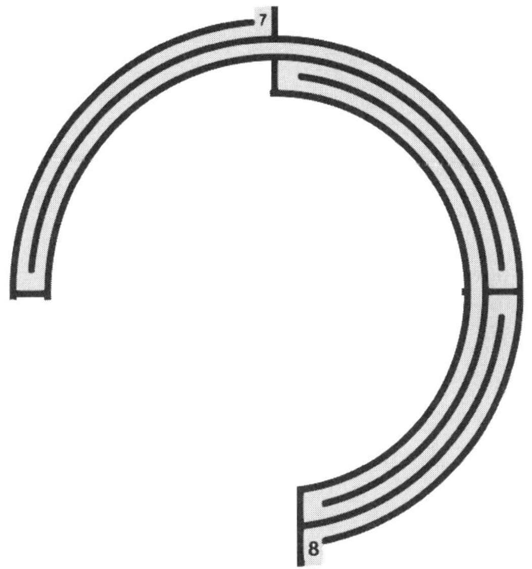

Step Eight requires a short surrender (down and to the left) which symbolizes a change in one's self-concept to accommodate the new experience of reality. Then there is a long journey in the heart to fully explore the new ability to receive guidance through one's heart about the purpose of one's life. It leads to a point near the beginning of the path but on the right side, indicating a surrender of the heart, like the surrender of the mind in Step Six. The mind is now convinced that its place is in service to the heart, and the heart takes its place as a reflection of the Universal Heart. For this reason, Step Eight is called the step of the "disciple."

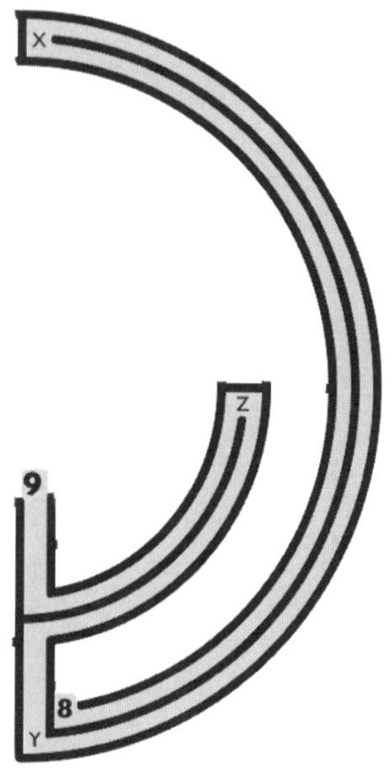

Step 9

The last step is entirely in the heart as it rises to the greatest height (X) and dives into the deepest depth (Y). After one final attunement (Z), one emerges into the center of the labyrinth, the fulfillment of the path of human development.

Chapter 9

Step 1: Commitment

THE FIRST THREE STEPS IN THE PATH of heart development prepare the mind, which we consider to be the surface of the heart, and strengthen the mind so it can perform its powerful and essential task: **concentration**. In steps four through six, we will use this power of concentration to focus the mind into the depth of the heart, diving deep into the essence of being to harness the infinite power we find there.

The first step in concentration is choosing one thing to concentrate upon. You have to first decide where to put your focus—this is setting an intention. Then the second step will be to hold your focus there in spite of distractions.

Your intention matures into a **commitment** when you realize that saying "Yes" to one thing is saying "No" to everything else. Concentration is a single focus. When you choose a college, a job or a lover, you choose only one. It is the singularity of the choice that makes it so powerful and important. It's your commitment that brings you the rewards of your activity.

- Committing to a relationship gives you a level of intimacy that comes from the safety of dedication.
- Committing to a job makes you one of the team and builds trust.
- Committing to the study of one subject can make you an expert.
- Committing to one instrument in the orchestra is the only way to world-class performance.
- Committing to one method of self-development gives you time to master it.

Yet many people are unable to make a commitment.

You surely know people who can't commit to a monogamous relationship. Some people can't work for an employer because they cannot commit to showing up on time, following orders and working for prescribed goals. Many people won't commit to a specific church, political party or service organization. A commitment is binding; why would you do that to yourself?

Everyone you know wants your attention, and once a relationship is formed, your commitment. Religious leaders want your commitment to their dogmas; political figures want your commitment to their party; bosses want your commitment to their goals. But what is your own commitment?

Choosing Your Commitment

The first step on the path requires the internal confidence to make a decision and follow it. When you can take this step of commitment, it is a cause for celebration. When you commit yourself, you might make the wrong choice, but you will realize it and then you will know more than you did before. If you make no choice, you will not be able to even start the path.

Even if you are convinced that a commitment is necessary, it can be difficult to choose one thing to which to give your focus. One student, in the midst of a difficult decision, told us: "I must choose what is best for me." This is a generally held notion: that our choices should be made based on what is most likely to bring us happiness.

But how do you know what is best for you? If only you could judge this better in advance, before committing. Your best indication about the rightness of a commitment is the way it turns out; if it turns out well, then you must have made the right decision. But this is like driving while looking in the rearview mirror. How can you know before you make a decision whether it will bring happiness or not?

The step of commitment requires the ability to make a choice without needing to know exactly what will happen. Of course you would like to have all the information needed to make a rational decision such as the destination and the obstacles, or the result and the cost, but such information seldom exists. All your interesting decisions occur when you are information-deprived, for example the choice of a lifelong lover, a business partner, or a spiritual teacher. When you make such a choice you demonstrate your state of being, your priorities and your access to intuition. You get the lover, the partner, and the teacher you deserve, and you yourself establish your worthiness. You make your evaluations based on those aspects of reality of which you are aware and which you value. The choice you make is your most sincere statement.

Making a commitment is saying, "I will," and the significance of saying these two words is enormous. It is repeating the vow we made in pre-eternity that began our process of individuation: the act of volunteering to come into human form for some purpose. Ever since that first act, we have practiced saying "I will" in many ways, each time strengthening our ability to begin and to follow through.

It's your commitments that define what you're about as a person, not your thoughts that come and go. If you want to know a person, find out what they're committed to.

If you're married, your marriage is a commitment. Perhaps you've committed to a monogamous relationship; that's a commitment. Deciding to be someone's friend is a commitment too. Joining a company is a commitment; taking initiation in a spiritual school is a commitment.

You do make commitments, and your commitments set in motion a series of activities and events that define a period of your life. You make a commitment, then that commitment makes you.

It's your commitments that determine how you'll spend your most precious resource: your time. Conversely, look at how you spend your time, and you'll see what you're tacitly committed to, even if you haven't formalized or recognized it.

Commitment Difficulties

There are also those who over-commit and try to develop two relationships or work at two careers or follow two paths at the same time. That is a failure of commitment that shows lack of confidence and weakness of concentration.

There are those who commit early, and there are those who commit late. For example, in a political campaign, those who endorse a candidate early in the race are the most loyal and committed supporters. They take the biggest risk because the outcome is far from certain. Those who endorse a candidate toward the end of the race are less sincere; they want to be counted with the winner, with minimum risk. Their commitment is still helpful, but had it come earlier they would have had a longer period of influence.

What if you commit to a friendship and your friend turns out to be a liability to you, like Barack Obama's ex-pastor, Jeremiah Wright? You can't foresee what the outcome will be when you take that step forward.

You take a step that you think is right at the time, but actually you cannot know with certainty if that step will help you or hurt you, or both. You take the step anyway, and that is the greatness in it. If you did know what would happen, any fool could decide whether to do it or not. The greatness in making a commitment is that it's a leap into the unknown.

Hazrat Inayat Khan says it's like stepping into the ocean for the first time. Who knows what dangers lurk in those breakers—there could be riptides, jellyfish, sea urchins, hidden rocks—and what joy you might experience bobbing on the waves.

Committing to a Spiritual Path

> In the East one will rarely find people taking the spiritual path without the guidance of a teacher, for there it is an accepted fact that these first three steps at least must be taken with the help of someone living a human life on earth. We can trace in the traditions that all the

> prophets, masters, saints, and sages, however great, had an initiator. In the life of Jesus Christ one reads that he was baptized by John the Baptist; and in the lives of all the other prophets and seers there was always someone, however humble or modest or human, and very often not at all comparable in greatness to those prophets, who took these first three steps with them.
>
> But the mother is really the first initiator of all the prophets and teachers in the world; no prophet or teacher, no saint, however great, was ever born who first walked alone without the help of the mother; she had to show him how to walk.[21]

In the spiritual path in the West, the inability or unwillingness to commit to a path is so common it's seen as preferable. Many prefer to gather spiritual wisdom like picking flowers, and with so many flowers available, the idea of specializing seems to be an undesirable limitation. This is a misunderstanding fed by fear of commitment. Choosing a path is not like limiting yourself to one kind of flower, for the genuine spiritual teacher will use whatever method is needed, and knows of more variety than the student imagines. Joining a spiritual school is like having a basket in which to put the flowers. A school is a container that holds all the spiritual knowledge, and makes sense of it by presenting one flower at a time, in the proper sequence.

Avoiding the commitment to one spiritual path hinders your progress. When you fall in love, you wish to spend your life with the beloved. When you study brain surgery, you seek out the best faculty and are very happy to devote yourself to that work. The spiritual path is as attractive as

---

[21] Hazrat Inayat Khan, Vol. 10, The Path of Initiation and Discipleship, 1. The Path of Initiation, 1st Initiation

falling in love and as complex as brain surgery. You wouldn't want to learn brain surgery from someone who also teaches plumbing, and it's heart-breaking to be separated from the one you love, even if you're surrounded by other attractive people.

Examples of Commitments

Here are some milestones from Puran's life that may help you in identifying your own milestones:

> *My first commitment was to science. As a young boy I was fascinated with electronics and learned how to fix radios. I pursued this interest in college. Then, in 1966, as a college senior, I had an intense spiritual awakening. With no precedent in my family, I became a dedicated pacifist in the beginning years of the Vietnam War. I joined the Quakers; my commitment to Christianity became the center of my life and led me to marry the woman I had been dating for five years. My love for religion overcame my love for science when two years later I quit the Ph. D. program I had almost completed to make a full-time commitment to the peace movement.*
>
> *I pressed my wife to have a child, my daughter. Often, the decision to have a child would be a significant inner change for a person, a commitment to a life-long responsibility. But for me, it was a part of my commitment to the peace movement, which I had already made. I expected to be put in prison, and the only marriages of men in my situation that survived prison were ones that had a child. So my first child was not a new commitment as much as an aspect of my existing commitment. I didn't go to prison, but nevertheless, the marriage didn't last.*
>
> *By 1971, my commitment to religion and peace had developed into a search for real mystical experience, which led me to the Sufis. In July of that year I found my teacher and took initiation, a commitment to discipleship that began another segment of my life. Discipleship is a rare experience in this culture, one*

that is vastly underrated and misunderstood. For me, it was incredibly fulfilling.

My period of discipleship continued for 33 years, but within the first year, I was asked to begin teaching. After considerable resistance, I committed to building a spiritual school as a natural outgrowth of my decision to accept a teacher. Being recognized as a teacher changed my relationship with my friends, my fellow seekers, and ultimately with my second wife. She had made the transition with me from the peace movement to mysticism and had eagerly embraced the same teacher. But she was not a teacher yet, and didn't understand the responsibility I was carrying.

My son Asatar was born in 1973, and my son Kahlil two years later, which added a further commitment to supporting a larger family. My academic period came to a complete end in 1975 when, at the request of my teacher, I left a prestigious research lab to help found his spiritual community. But leaving the lab and moving to a rural community was not the milestone; the milestone was my commitment to building a spiritual school, which had occurred in 1972. It took a few more years to cause a change in my life's circumstances, but those changes were an inevitable product of the commitment.

My second divorce was another outcome of my commitment to building a spiritual school (a complicated story). I was glad to have custody of one of my three children, but separation from the other two caused intense, heart-attack-like pains in my chest. Following my commitments to support my family and build a spiritual school, I took a well-paying job and taught classes in meditation in the evenings and early mornings.

In 1977, just after leaving the spiritual community I had helped found, I had an inner experience of great power. This dramatic development, with the encouragement of my teacher, caused me to reduce the time I spent teaching to begin a new chapter of high-risk, high-value projects as an inventor and entrepreneur. I worked extremely hard in industrial and financial companies, still teaching and practicing meditation.

There were many more turns to come, but from my story so far I hope you can see that it's our inner changes that cause us to change our outer circumstances. The inner changes tend to revolve around new commitments: for me, it was first my commitment to science; then to Christianity, the peace movement, mystical training; building a spiritual school, and all the while supporting my family.

Truly, your commitments, freely made as an act of will, define your priorities in life and each new commitment divides your life's story into chapters.

Consider, what are some commitments you have made? How have your commitments defined the chapters of your life?

Here is another story of commitment, from a student in one of our courses on The Map:

I am starting to suspect that I may have actually been avoiding commitment all along, in many areas. It seems there is a difference between commitment and working your guts out for something. I'm trying to walk two or three spiritual paths. I'm still trying to make theatre and dreaming of a theatre company.

Everything these last two weeks has been pointing to a lack of mastery, and to what real mature mastery in teaching, meditation, and spiritual practice might look like and feel like. I am afraid of missing out, wanting to do everything. On my request, a friend confronted and challenged me about my integrity in dealing with the things I had on my plate. He said: Look, I want you to go to work, do an honest eight hours and leave a tidy desk. I committed to it. My energy today has been so much cleaner and clearer. I am feeling how committing could simplify my life and actually allow me to live as a more whole being, with less ragged flailing. It's quite an experiential revelation. I can see that my pattern has been to try to marry each new love without divorcing the old. I thought that the loyal thing was not to abandon the prior commitment, and I have tried to synthesize. But truly doing this means I am unable to maintain integrity with the commitments I already have. Today, I felt the energy and integrity that came from operating from commitment, and it makes me realize that it might be possible to live in an unfragmented way in the world. Raggedly flailing about takes a lot of energy.

Saying "I will" or, worse, "I will commit" seems so odd right now. On what grounds? I'm thinking, 'I want to know the All, to be one with the Universe in all its facets and depth: why would anyone deliberately narrow their focus?' I can imagine doing it with humor, playfully, as a player in the cosmic drama, or a buffoon in the divine comedy. But what about all the other roles? Some actors like to go from one project to the next. My ideal has been to be in a company which keeps plays in its repertoire for decades, and I'd play a variety of roles for a long time, going into each of them deeply. Like having a harem! How do people choose? Raggedness will force a choice and maybe should have before now. Right now, I remain a rabbit in the headlights of this call to singular commitment.

Another student's story of commitment follows:

Yesterday I opened to the pain of the ending of my first marriage. I cheated on my husband three times during our 17-year marriage and told him each time. The third time, which is when I left, was a soap opera scenario. I so believed in what I was doing that I shut out the pain I was creating for myself and others, most significantly my husband and son. Yesterday, I allowed myself to remember the day my six-foot-tall, 200-pound 17-year old leapt onto my lap when I told him I was leaving. Holding him on my 115-pound frame, feeling the sharpness of the pain searing through my body, I 'flicked the switch' as I had done so many times growing up. In that moment I could not face his pain nor mine. I wanted what I wanted, which was a different man.

I'm not even sure that I ever made a conscious commitment to be a wife and mother. I got myself pregnant at 20 (I thought I knew how not to get pregnant) and, ashamed, allowed everyone else to shuffle me through the process of marriage and birth. Once my son was born I fell in love with him and was a very good, attentive and loving mother. Yes – I was committed then. We read book after book on child rearing; I was committed to giving him a different upbringing than I had.

One year ago on Mother's Day weekend, my current husband told me he was in love with another woman and left me. I was devastated! One week later, he asked for forgiveness and a new commitment. We threw our wedding rings in the ocean; today, we are doing Heart Rhythm Meditation together, and consciously choose to wear no symbol on our fingers to show ourselves or others our marriage commitment. Instead, we share a process, a continuous growth and deepening of our love and understanding of each other. Where that will take us, for me, is unknown. I am committed to be in the moment and process of what it is right now, which is healing and loving.

A story of commitment from Susanna:

When we emigrated from Hungary when I was 4, I felt, "Great. Now the journey starts." I was not sad about leaving our home, I was enthusiastic about it. I had some premonition that I should be going west. I kept moving west in my life, from Hungary to Austria, Switzerland, Germany, New York, and now Tucson, Arizona.

When I was 10, I asked my mother to send me to a Catholic boarding school. I had been in a middle-school and when it came time for us to take the test that sets the whole direction of a person's life, whether to go on to a college-prep high school or to a vocational high school, my teacher wouldn't even let me take the test. So my only way to prepare for college was to go to the Catholic school. My mother agreed.

At this age, I could see that if I didn't go on to college, my life's scope would be very limited. So I made a commitment to get to college. For nine years I persisted in the Catholic boarding school, even though the nuns wanted to expel me three times, for being too much of a challenge. This commitment, which I worked hard to keep, gave me a ticket to life — the opportunity to study at the University of Vienna.

Make a Commitment Now

> Take your well-disciplined strengths and stretch them between two great opposing poles... Because inside human beings is where God learns. —Rainer Maria Rilke[22]

A commitment should be specific, clear and objective so you can easily remember and affirm it. A commitment is not the same as a goal. A goal is in the future; a commitment is in the present. For example:

"I commit to establishing a daily practice of Heart Rhythm Meditation."

"I commit to creating (or strengthening) a relationship with _____."

"I commit to the path of the heart."

You may find yourself wanting to make more than one commitment, but making a single commitment is more effective. With some thought, you should be able to embody all of your minor commitments under the umbrella of a major

---

[22] Rilke in Bly (2005).

commitment. "I commit to eating less sugar and quitting smoking" could be transformed into "I commit to treat my body with the care and generosity it deserves."

Some commitments people have shared with us:

- I commit to being centered in myself and keeping my heart open and staying on my heart path all the time I can – even when others are personally critical of me.
- I commit to deepening my relationship to my spouse.
- I commit to becoming aware of my conduct towards others and myself in the words I use. Are they what the heart would want spoken?
- I commit to improving my relationship with my sister, and developing compassion for her.
- I commit to honoring the mystery of the beloved in my partner.
- I commit to keeping refined sugar, white flour, rice and pasta to the barest minimum.
- I commit to plan and work on my office (my own space where I don't need to solicit input from my partner) and the front entry of my home, which is not very welcoming right now.
- I commit to living a life of balance by fully exercising my body, mind and heart on a daily basis.

What commitment would you like to make at this time in regards to a relationship, your work, your health, or your spiritual practice?

Chapter 10
Step 2: Testing

If you wish to probe the depths of a person's character, test him or her with that which is his or her life's greatest need. —Hazrat Inayat Khan

THE FIRST SIX STEPS OF THE PATH develop the individual self. The steps beyond that develop the transpersonal aspects of the self. In developing the individual self, the first three steps develop the mind, the next three steps develop the heart.

"Yes" and "No."

The development of your mind gives you the ability to (1) direct your attention to one object, (2) hold your attention on that object, and then (3) relate to that object, observing it intently, understanding it and operating it. These three steps give will-power, the power of the mind.

With this power, your mind forms a personal boundary defined by the area that receives your attention. All your interests and relationships are within this area of attention. It is a unique area; no one else has directed their mind over exactly the same field of ideas, so the area of your attention *defines* your individuality.

As seekers of the heart, we are trying to erase the boundaries that divide and limit people, but first we must create those boundaries to define people as individuals. Before our human life, as angels of light we had no boundaries because angels are not distinct from each other. It was the first "I will," proclaimed in the time before life, that started the process of individuation. This process must be brought to a conclusion, to a focus, in order to finally ground the soul in a psyche, just as the body grounds the soul in physicality. Later we will expand the boundaries of self until they burst, but first we must form a powerful center that can hold the self together without a boundary. That center is the heart.

So the first step is to declare your will, which is commitment, and the second step is to affirm that will, which we call testing. The first step is to say "yes," the second step is to say "no." The third step balances the "yes" and "no" to give understanding, trust and harmony.

Living on earth is like living in a supermarket where everything you could possibly want is available. As you choose what to put in your basket of attention, you define who you are. To some things you say, "yes," to other things you say "no," and what you say "yes" to one day you will say "no" to another day. Because your basket is only so big, the objects you choose to put in it will push other objects out. Some objects that fall out will be invited back later, and some objects which receive a lot of attention now will later receive none.

It is very exciting to say "yes," whereas "no" is painful and confining. It's obvious that "yes" must be the first step;

if you started with "no" you could not continue. But if you always say "yes," you show no discrimination, no individuality. It is your "no" that creates the boundary of your self.

The Value of Tests

Step Two continues the development of concentration that was begun in Step One, by building the strength to exclude all the diversions that pull your attention away from your focus point. Diversions are the tests of your interest and commitment; they are provided plentifully so you can demonstrate, by ignoring them, the priority of your commitment.

> The imitation of gold can be as beautiful as real gold; the imitation of the diamond as bright as a real diamond. The difference is that one fails in the test of endurance, and the other can stand it. Yet one must not be compared to objects. People have something divine in themselves, and they can prove this by their endurance in the path of love. —HIK[23]

This is an even-numbered step. The path alternates from the right foot to the left foot as we take one step in glory (the odd-numbered steps) and the next step in surrender (the even-numbered steps). The surrender in Step Two is all you give up by focusing on the object of concentration. Concentration requires focus, and everything else falls out of focus.

- A commitment in marriage requires exclusivity.
- In working for an employer, one gives up conflicts of interest.

---

[23] Hazrat Inayat Khan, Social Gathekas, 17. Sufi Mysticism, III: Preparing the Heart for the Path of Love

- One cannot take medicine from two different doctors unless they are in close collaboration. Likewise, one should not mix two spiritual practices unless the combination is prescribed by a master of both.

  You are tested and you test others.

- The teacher tests the students to determine if their commitment is real.
- The student tests the teacher to determine what are the teacher's strengths and limitations.
- The beloved tests the lover to determine the strength of his/her love.
- Life itself tests us. Make a boast or a claim, and something will surely occur to test that statement. Every commitment, every resolution, and every decision will be tested.
- Your abilities will be tested by your challenges.
- Your understanding will be tested by your problems.
- Your loyalty will be tested by your acceptance.

Every skill, ability and quality must be tested by your ability to apply them so that you can make these resources conscious and develop them further.

Testing can be strengthening or it can be weakening. If you pass the test you feel confirmed. If you don't pass the test that is given, then you must either pull back or make a further commitment, going through the first step again. A further commitment will require further testing. Hence, you may cycle through the first and second steps many times.

Step Two expresses that aspect of you that is the disbeliever, the cynic and the skeptic, in contrast to that aspect that is expressed in the first step: the courageous risk-taker and dedicated loyalist. Some people have the tendency to step out and then see where they are, while others have the need to investigate and question before moving. You have both parts really, and your courage and your caution argue with each other like kids that get married too early. You break up and try again, with the same person or another version of that person until you can appreciate both courage and caution.

There is love in being tested and confirmed. In a relationship, you test a person to see how they will respond in a certain situation. If the one you love passes the test in front of your friends, you test him/her in front of your parents. But there are always more tests you could make. How will (s)he respond when you are sick? When you are angry, or depressed? Will the other be jealous of a third? Will the one you love help your career or sabotage it? There are so many questions—just how far does the other's commitment go? Testing is the only way to answer these questions. So your relationship will remain in the step of testing for as long as it takes—maybe many decades—for you to satisfy yourself that you know the other person through so many situations that you can trust them in the untested situations. Basically, you get tired of testing, and you just stop it.

Testing in the Spiritual Work

> There are tests of many kinds that the teacher may give to his pupil to test his faith, his sincerity, his patience. Before a ship puts to sea the captain goes and makes sure that everything is in order for the voyage; and such is the duty of the teacher.—HIK

Another important relationship is that which develops between a student and a spiritual teacher. Just as a teacher tests a student, a student tests a teacher and his or her teachings: "Is the teacher genuine? Does she have my interest at heart, or is she trying to get something from me? Do these teachings make sense to me? Am I growing and learning?"As teachers ourselves, we know it's important to test anyone who would make the audacious claim of being a teacher!

Regarding the relationship with the teacher, Hazrat Inayat Khan wrote about the questioning of the second step:

> Some did say that I knew nothing,
> Some still held that I knew all.
> Some did turn their back to me, and
> Some quickly answered my call.
>
> Some on hearing my words exclaimed, "Nothing he said that was new." Some said, "I have always thought this; That is my own point of view."
>
> Some asked, "What mystery he revealed? What wonder did he perform?" Some answered, "We ask no wonder, so long as his heart is warm."
>
> Some said, "He is a man as we are, what difference in him do you see?" Some answered, "It is not to know; what is needed, is to be."

It is not the brilliant articulation, nor the knowledge of esoterica, nor even miraculous interventions that prove a person to be a teacher. The proof is in the one thing that cannot be faked: the atmosphere of his being.

The relationship with the teacher is of a different kind than other relationships. Although the spiritual teacher is like a sibling, a parent and a friend, she is none of those. People alternately underestimate and overestimate the teacher, who is neither a person like themselves nor a wonder-worker from heaven, and who is both very ordinary and quite extraordinary. The teacher cannot be understood by observation, only by contemplation, but that skill doesn't develop until Step Four in the path (and is only really accessible then if you have learned a method for it, which is unusual). All you see at this step is your own projection onto the mirror of the teacher's heart. The teacher is playing Cupid to attract you toward yourself. Can you trust this process without understanding it?

Step Two is also occurring with regard to your practice of Heart Rhythm Meditation. At this point there is a predictable reaction to your concentration on your heart. Your heart will have responded to your *attention*, your breath's *inspiration* and your *intention*, and will have produced strong and surprising experiences of energy, emotion and vision. You may be frightened by these experiences, which are only a taste of what's to come, or you might dismiss them as fantasy.[24] You might become so fascinated by the experiences themselves that you overlook their meaning. This is your test: are you ready to answer the call of your heart or will you turn away until later in your life?

There is another way you will test the path: after you find the practices really work and help you, you will wonder, "Can I be the same as I was? What will happen if I *don't* do the practices?" Consequently, you will suspend your meditation for some time, as a test. You'll then find that life doesn't go as well, and hopefully you'll resume your meditation.

> *A great spiritual teacher in India was renowned for his teachings; he taught that true worship is of the invisible, formless*

---

[24] See the Six Basic Powers, Bair and Bair (2007), pp 98-105

unity that pervades all beings and all forms. He had a thousand devoted pupils. One day, he told them he had decided to go and bow before Kali, a Hindu goddess with a definite form and specific qualities. His pupils, among them many doctors, professors and other esteemed, intelligent people, found this difficult to swallow. It went against all they thought they knew: that they should worship the formless, not some statue. Their confidence in their teacher was destroyed. All his disciples walked away, save one young man who was very devoted to his teacher.

As the teacher and his one remaining student walked to the temple of Kali, the teacher tried to persuade the disciple to leave him as the others did. The student refused and continued to walk with his teacher. On the way, the teacher's heart became full as he thought about human nature: how fickle it can be, how a single statement can change a relationship. He was so full of feeling that when he reached the temple of Kali, he reached a state of ecstasy, and this ecstasy brought him to fall before the statue of the goddess and bow his head. His student did the same.

After the two had gotten up, the teacher asked again, "Why do you follow me?" The young man replied that he had seen nothing in his teacher's conduct that went against what he has been teaching; that it matters not at all what one bows before, as the same Oneness exists in all things. This young man had been the only one, out of all the learned adherents who studied under this teacher, who was able to receive this lesson.

Teachers test their pupils in many ways. Academic teachers test students' knowledge, cognitive ability, reasoning skills, and ability to communicate. Spiritual teachers test their students' faith, sincerity, and patience. Such tests are often given to students who have reached a point where they know a lot—where their knowledge seems perhaps to have filled them to a point where they are closed to new teachings. Such tests may be posed when a teacher relays something to a student that seems, on the outside, to mean one thing while the inner meaning is quite different; the test, then, is about the student being able to perceive both—a sign that he or she is no longer only seeing things on their surface, but is gaining a deeper perspective.

Every teacher of any kind knows that it is a great joy to see a student pass a test. It gives the student a powerful, direct experience of being recognized, confirmed and found worthy. The test is a gift of the teacher to the student— provided that the teacher is careful to properly assess the strengths of the student and to give a test that will push the student, provoking growth, and a test that the student can pass.

Wise spiritual teachers know how to test their students without even letting on that it's a test. The teacher makes a request, then observes the response. If the test is passed, a more important request is given and the response to that is felt. The student who is ready may find himself tested more and more severely. This testing serves the universe by showing it which of us can be counted on; the student grows through this process, much more rapidly and fully then he or she would have without the teacher.

Tests in Love

Tests of commitment do not only come from spiritual teachers. We are tested continually in our lives, by events, relationships, and choices. In a love relationship, for example, you test your partner. Will he come when called? Will she be understanding in the face of your needs? Will he value what you find sacred? Will she maintain her commitment to you when you aren't around? By these tests, trust is built.

When we are confident in a person's love, we can endure times when that love may seem to be absent or limited. We build that confidence by experience over time. The process of becoming confident in a person's love is what we mean by the word "testing," which admittedly sounds unappealing. Eventually we are able to remain confident of God's Love even through times that we do not understand, when we feel betrayed and broken and alone. God develops our confidence in God, called "faith," by testing us, gently and with infinite love.

If you cannot pass the tests you are given, you must break your commitment and fall back to Step One with a new, different commitment. If you can pass the test, then you pass on to the third step. Testing can be strengthening or it can be weakening. If you pass the test, you feel confirmed. If you don't pass the test that is given, then you must either pull back or make a further commitment, going through the first step again. A further commitment will require further testing. **You may cycle through the first and second steps many times, and there is no harm in this.** Continuing along the path is what matters; you can't move into the next step until you are truly ready.

Examples of Real-Life tests

Asatar Bair, a teacher and mentor in IAM, has an example of testing:

> *When I was hired as a professor of economics, I made a series of poor decisions early on—decisions that alienated members of my tenure committee and nearly got me fired. In retrospect, I was testing my desires, the direction I had chosen, and my ideals with regard to teaching and contributing to economic*

theory. When I was in graduate school, I tested my teachers and my friends alike; after confronting and alienating much of the faculty, I had a conflict with two professors who later became my dissertation advisors. They were requiring me to take an additional exam, which I felt was unnecessary and even designed to intimidate me. I asked my friends to come and support me outside the hall right before the exam. My professors weren't sure if it was just support or a kind of picket line. (In retrospect, it was a bit of both.) They gave me the benefit of the doubt, but it was a close thing. I almost lost the only support I had from the faculty. That would've been the end of my academic career right there.

Paula Roome, a teacher in IAM, wrote about her testing:

I have been angry since reading about Step 2, the testing process. I find it hard to write; in my head, it bubbles over. I sit down and no words will flow. I am angry when I read people's postings and Puran's answers. I am failing completely with the Square Breath;[25] *I do not fully exhale and inhale, which seems to demonstrate my lack of trust in my life. I have gone back to working on my full in- and exhalations, but still, I can only feel my heart beat on my right side; the left has no feeling! Today, the feeling of failure is in there big time. I know I test people but now I am being tested and I don't like it at all. Puran, I can almost hear you laugh, "Great stuff, keep at it, you're really being tested!" I will post again after I have either exploded or calmed down.*

A musician's story of testing:

I'm afraid of tests—really afraid. At the mention of the word 'test' I freeze in the belief that I'm going to get it wrong. The other side of my dread of being wrong is the need to be 'right,' even about trivial matters. If I'm not right, I'm nothing! Un-

---

[25] For the details on this practice, see *Living from the Heart*, pp 188-194

less I'm told I'm a genius at something, I've failed. Mind you, being told I'm a genius only gets me to the point of feeling OK. This is the 'high ego, low self-esteem' paradigm. Even trivial tests are big tests for me. Sometimes everything feels like a test. After I 'fail' or 'get it wrong' I have a strong desire to give up all hope of living in the world—to resign myself to the fact that it's all too hard. I tend to feel things in such extremes.

To avoid failure, I 'test the waters' of any new group of people before committing to a suitable persona. Once established in the group, I tire of the persona I've formulated to try to avoid being wrong or making a mistake. I end up feeling trapped in it—as if forced into a false 'me'—and self-hatred sets in. Sometimes, motivated by this self-hatred, I physically move on to another place, where I think I'll have a 'blank slate' again, without all the pretense of that persona I had invented to fit in. Within six weeks of moving to a new place, I would find that I again had invented a tailor-made persona, just for that group! People used to love these invented Davids; if competing groups or individuals met by chance, I was put in the uncomfortable position of needing to be two different people at the same time – a very difficult test of 'who am I really?'

Puran has a story of a female friend whose great aspiration was to be married:

Sandra and I worked at the same company in our late twenties, and I had been married for two years. During our friendship she began a relationship that led to marriage. All along, as it deepened, she shared her anxiety with me: "Would he really accept me if he knew all about me?" She worried that she couldn't really count on him to help her if she fell into despair. Immediately after the wedding, she gave him the test that was required: she sunk into despair and had to be hospitalized. Her new husband fled. Later, he returned, but her trust of him was not restored. Later the marriage failed.

She had erred in keeping up a front throughout the courtship that hid the parts of herself that she feared. If he could have met those aspects of her in the context of her strengths, he would have known they were manageable. In seeing that he could manage them, she might have come to know that they were manageable, too.

Here is the story of a woman in one of our courses:

I really love the progression into the Testing step as I can see it very clearly in my life.

The most prominent and pressing example of testing is unrequited love. It will be almost a year since we last saw each other (my birthday). She left me. I continue loving her. The way I think I'm tested now, after all this time, has to do with knowing when to keep or let go of hope that she'll return. I spend so much time simply loving her in my heart and mind; that will not go away. But I'm wondering if it's time to let go of the part that dreams of our being together again.

What is it with me that my beloved ones leave me? It's a painful and lonely experience. I keep on loving them and I know they care for me too, but for some reason, neither one of us can communicate in a way that would clear space and give room for understanding and forward movement for our relationship. I'm pretty good and courageous with directly communicating from my heart, but for some reason, I've failed with these beautiful people.

I can see this in operation all the time in my life. As soon as one comes to stand for something, along comes a test to that stand. Reaffirming my stands strengthens not only the stand, but my belief in myself. I love this whole process.

Several of our students have had some history, either past or present, of same-sex relationships, and in their stories we feel the pain of same-sex loves not being accepted by important people in their lives or by the culture. From a spiritual point of view, the soul, heart and mind all have the same gender, neither male or female, but the gender of the body is determined by circumstances at the moment of conception that are not under the control of the soul. Perhaps this is why some people feel that their physical gender or desire is not suited to their soul, heart and mind. Very few people notice this mismatch because the physical identity is so strong and the soul identity is unconscious for all but a few.

Reflections on Step Two

> How have you tested your parent's love, the commitment of your lover, the rightness of your job, the integrity of a friend?
>
> How have you been tested?

For example: what was it that made you know for certain that you would marry the person you were dating? The courtship is a period of testing preceded by a commitment and followed by a further commitment of marriage. Then the marriage commitment has to be tested.

What made you know you had found the right job or career?

In a relationship that ultimately failed, can you see what tested it?

How have you been benefited by testing?

Chapter 11
Step 3: Harmony

> If one endures through all the tests then comes the third step, the third initiation. The third initiation consists of three stages: receiving the knowledge attentively; meditating upon all one has received patiently; assimilating all the outcome of it intelligently. —HIK

OUR MAP OF ADULT DEVELOPMENT has reached the end of the first major stage, the development of the mind. Notice that we've never once mentioned intelligence in this discussion of mental development; instead, our discussion has been about the development of concentration. Intelligence takes different forms: mathematical intelligence, musical intelligence, intuitive intelligence, and so on. Even people with a high level of intelligence need to learn how to focus their mind so that their intelligence can be utilized.

Concentration begins with commitment, is developed by testing and results in knowledge and success. All accomplishments require concentration; even asking for something requires concentration. Having demonstrated your ability to choose an object of concentration through commitment, and to define the boundary of your attention through the "no" of testing, you are rewarded by a continual flow of information coming from the object of your concentration. As you process this information over time, you develop knowledge.

Sometimes the information flow between you and the object of your attention is very brief, like opening a shutter on a camera, while the development time is much longer, like the chemical development of photographic film. A brief glance can pass so much information that it takes a decade to process it. Or the information flow coming through concentration can be very long, like the exposure to a person in a relationship, and suddenly result in knowing that person.

The first three steps are on a flat dance floor. We spin around and around, dancing from Step One to Step Two; Step One, Step Two, until we are thoroughly satisfied with testing and re-committing and we sit down and observe the dance in understanding.

Let's examine what it is that makes these three steps important milestones in life. Early in life you realize that every person, every organization and every cause wants your commitment. A psychologist would say that everyone wants your attention, but attention can be fleeting. *Sustained* attention comes from commitment. Commitment is the act of saying "I will", and this is the great power given to the human being, the ability to individuate the will of the universe. Spiritually, we see that what everyone wants from you is your magical power of being able to focus the attention of the universe. Your concentration brings the universe into focus on the object of your attention, just as you are yourself a focus of the universe.

- There is a saying, "Man proposes, God disposes." What you think of, with consistency and intention, draws the attention of God.
- Jesus Christ said, "What you allow on earth shall be allowed in heaven, and what you forbid on earth shall be forbidden in heaven." For this to be true, you must be able to focus the attention of God.

We can see then, that "I will" is the ultimate power; it commits the resources of the universe. In the old language we would say, "'I will' binds the hand of God." Anything can be accomplished by the magic of commitment, and since we all sense this, every cause tries to gather your commitment.

Many people are frightened of the power of "I will," and resist giving their commitment. Others give their commitment easily, which then dilutes its power. Because an individual's commitment is so cosmically significant, it must be verified. That is the process of *testing*, to confirm what you committed to. Does this new commitment you've made have priority over the last commitment you made? What are the boundaries of this commitment? If you've committed to make more money, for example, is it by any means or are some means unacceptable? If you've committed to a relationship, is it irrespective of how you are treated by the other?

In testing, you will discover much about the meaning of the commitment you made. Often, you will discover you made the wrong commitment: it wasn't exactly what you intended. Say you want to make more money, but you also want the respect of your peers and the blessing of your conscience. Then you are not actually committed to making money; you're committed to having an honest, respectable career. If you want closeness and affection, but not blame and confinement, then the open-ended commitment of marriage isn't really what you want; you actually are committing to the giving and receiving of affection.

When your commitment is confirmed and the boundary of your commitment is determined by testing, then the results begin to flow. The universe will deliver what you requested of it. Thus we call Step Three *Harmony.*

The realization of Step Three is that while you can have anything you concentrate upon, you will have to pay for it by sacrificing something else you also want. The lament, "Why can't I have what I want?" is answered: because you also want something else that conflicts with it. For example, perhaps you want (1) to make a lot of money, and (2) to not take advantage of anyone. That combination will take much longer for the universe to deliver than if you wanted just (1) alone, or just (2) alone.

In a few words, the first three steps can be expressed as:

1. "I will."
2. "I won't."
3. "I know."

Every time you make a new commitment, you take Step One again, and then you will have to go through Step Two again to test that commitment. But once you have reached Step Three, the first two steps can be repeated quickly and easily with new commitments. Even though you still have to begin a new job, a new relationship and a new path at Step One, there is permanent progress. Because you now have confidence in the process, you can readily attain Step Three in a new situation and gain new knowledge. Competency in any area gives confidence that can be applied to another area.

Step 3 at Work

In a job, with the competency and confidence that Step Three creates, you will be assured of success. Every aspect of your job is known now, and you can perform it very well, almost automatically. Surprises are few and results are reliable. You can quickly learn a new job skill and perform it as well as your old skill. Step Three, Harmony, is all about confidence and competency.

The movie *Peaceful Warrior* tells the story of an incredibly good gymnast who achieved his excellence by training with a master.[26] The lessons of his teacher were such as these:

- Bring your attention to the present moment.
- There is never nothing happening. (Awareness reveals a rich dynamism.)
- You have to take out the trash. (Empty your mind of all that distracts from the task of the moment.)
- Learn to listen to what others aren't saying.
- The journey is more important than the destination.

This is part of the teaching of Concentration, which is the first step toward Meditation. When concentration is attained, amazing things can be done. The secrets of life open to those who can hold their glance steady. The mind has a power that can demand a puzzle to yield its solution when you give the puzzle enough attention. Any question will

---

[26] Based on the book *Way of the Peaceful Warrior*. Millman (2006)

reveal its answer to a steady gaze.

> If I were to interpret the words of Christ, "Straight is the gate and narrow is the way", I would say that there is a path in life, a path of going straight, and that path is like walking upon a wire. In the circus they make a show of it. It is exactly the picture: at every step one takes there is fear of falling either to one side or to the other. Jugglers in India even make a better picture of it. They take two very light bamboos and tie a rope on the top of them. The juggler stands on the rope in a brass tray and her task is to go from one point to the other. While she is traveling thus, her colleagues from below beat drums and sing horrible songs in order to distract her mind. She has to keep her concentration and secure her balance in spite of all the music calling her from below. That is the picture of right living. — HIK[27]

Step 3 in Relationships

Step Three in a relationship gives acceptance and trust. You have tested your lover under so many different situations that their responses have become predictable. Their strengths and weaknesses are all known, at least in ordinary circumstances. You know how to aggravate the other person and what you can count on them for; you know their sensitivities and strengths. Therefor, there is no need for further testing. You trust what you know and accept the rest. You can't test every possible situation, so testing can never be complete. At some point you decide to stop testing and just trust.

There are those who, upon meeting someone new, withhold their trust until the person proves to be trustworthy.

[27] Hazrat Inayat Khan, Vol. 8, The Privilege of Being Human, 6. Man is likened to the Light

They have not attained Step Three; they have no confidence in their ability to know a person. Then there are those who, upon meeting someone new, extend their trust until the person proves to be untrustworthy. When you can trust first, without testing, you show Step Three. You have confidence that you know the other person sufficiently to extend trust. You may have a surprising disappointment, because there are secrets deep in a person's heart that cannot be seen from outside. Still, by trusting you will have learned more about a person than by continual testing.

Many people never get to this step. They may reach a guarded acceptance with a temporary suspension of testing until a new, untested, situation presents itself, but that is not the third step. Only those who have developed trust have come to this step. If one requires that everything about the other person be proven, there is no trust; there is only fact.

If you have fully trusted *anyone*, then you have attained this step. Once the ability to trust is developed, it will grow until it becomes the norm and then you can trust those you have not tested. At this step, you can endure even a severe disappointment without losing your ability to trust. Once love has reached the third step, it is possible to love again after a breakup. You know the beauty of the relationship you can reach through trust is so valuable that it justifies the risk you take by trusting.

Those who feel they have been fooled by another and can no longer trust are those who never did trust, they just got tired of testing. They have not reached the third step. After a disappointment they become bitter and consequently pull back from further commitment in the future. The inability to trust shows the person is still in the cycle of Step One,

Step Two. This is seen in the spiritual path when a student has become disappointed in a teacher and becomes resistant to all teachers thereafter, and in love relationships when one is hurt and resolves not to be vulnerable again. Such a person is very difficult to get close to. Unless they can make the third step, their life will be lonely. Their disappointment has raised the tests they give others to an unreachable height. The only way out is to find a trustworthy person, like a teacher, to whom they can give their trust as a way to practice trusting others.

The harmony of Step Three is because of trust.

The prickly pear cactus grows thorns on its succulent flesh to protect it from being eaten by animals. But when the cactus grows on the side of cliffs where it cannot possibly be reached by any animal, it drops its thorns. Luther Burbank, the mystical botanist, was able to develop a strain of cactus without thorns in his laboratory by telling his plants, "You don't need your thorns here, I will protect you."

Step Three allows you to thrive while being vulnerable and unprotected. There is no more need for thorns in your personality. You do not have to test people before you can trust them.

Step 3 in Spirituality

In our school, Step Three occurs when you have satisfied yourself that our method is valid, our teachers are genuine, and our school is effective. At this step you will have experienced your physical heart and found its heartbeat, and have controlled your breath to be rhythmic and full. You may have felt some pain in your heart, but still the practice feels safe. You have no more fear about where this path is going to take you, and you feel comfortable with all you have found. Your trust will enable you to progress quickly from here on.

The difficulty a student has at this step is that the student's understanding of the teacher and the path is based on external observation. Consequently, what the student sees in the teacher is almost entirely a projection. No one can be understood from the outside; to know a person requires insight by entering into their heart, a process we call *Contemplation,* which begins at Step Four. Concentration is seeing with the mind; contemplation is seeing and feeling with the heart. The mind's view gives the false impression that others are separate from yourself and that your observations can produce accurate and valid judgments of them.

At Step Three, people are not aware of the limitation of concentration, which can only give a superficial knowledge of the object of concentration. The understanding from concentration is useful, but it misses the nuances and the inner meaning of things. For example, because you've come to accept your own shortcomings, you can rationalize the mistakes and failures of others. "Everyone is human," you may say, completely missing the motivation behind an intentional act that you may interpret as a mistake. This is especially a problem with a teacher because you will assume that the teacher's motivation and intention is similar to your own.

> *A student once observed his teacher being fined at a customs checkpoint for not declaring an expensive tape recorder that was bought abroad. The student assumed the teacher's motive was similar to what his own would have been in that situation, trying to save the customs fee. But the teacher's thinking was completely different: he didn't mind contributing to the coffers of the state if that was the custom; there was no attempt to violate the law or save money. The teacher just doesn't relate*

to the concept of borders and so it did not occur to him that the people of one area would want to be paid for something that was already paid for in another area. His borderless consciousness could not be appreciated by his student who saw the situation through his own mental patterns.

In another case, a teacher who was running a small business interrupted a crucial development process to attend to the health condition of a minor investor in the company. The teacher was criticized by his employees for giving so much valuable attention to an investor who was not able to invest further. But the teacher knew this man represented a figure in a parable that was being re-enacted through his company and its quest. Certain classic patterns with symbolic and metaphorical power are repeated often in human affairs and when recognized, can be exploited. By helping this man heal the teacher was operating the power of an ancient drama that would unfold the next step in the company's success.

Examples of Step 3

The following is from a woman in one of our courses:

In regard to testing being over and behind us, it appears I have not reached Step 3. I am unsatisfied that the method is valid, teachers genuine and school effective. I am challenged not to be resistant to all teachers hereafter. I have also been hurt in a love relationship so I am also challenged to not refuse to be vulnerable again... a deep sigh.

Then, a few days later:

New day, new start. Inayat Khan says, "If by accident you step into the mud, it is not therefore necessary to walk in the muddy path." I see today that I do have someone I feel I am done testing and whom I can trust completely: myself. In my relationship with myself, I experience harmony and trust when I'm in rhythm with my heart and when I am honest with myself. I got here through observation followed by acceptance. I am going to keep trusting in this process at the risk of being pointed in the direction of the nearest insane asylum.

And again, after a few more days:

Today I came to the realization that there is only one relationship that leads to the goal, including the one that is causing me so much pain. And yes, I consistently fall, wanting more from the relationship, grasping, trying to hold and own the person, not recognizing the love that moves through us and between us, caught in the endless 'desire' self of wanting and owning. But then every so often, it's like an awakening happens, I come back to my heart, and this person is there, stable, strong and unmoved, breathing Perfect Love. So, I do feel I can trust this person completely due to our long association and deep bonding. My trust of this person has gotten me to this place of realizing how love for one person is also love for every person.

Here is a story of trust from Elijah Imlay, a teacher in our school:

My partner is never jealous of me or I of her. We have heated arguments and work through issues and misunderstandings, and this process strengthens our love. I have examined my life from her perspective and have learned much from her.

I trust my partner to tell the truth, to act with courage even when she feels afraid, to show integrity, to stand up for principles, to say the difficult things that need to be said even if she is disliked for saying them, to challenge me to be the best I can be, to support all aspects of my growth, to trust that I will never betray her trust, to love me unconditionally, to always ask for what she wants, to give generously of herself, to sacrifice herself for those she loves, to honor what is important to herself, to her students, and to the significant people in her life, to pay attention to important details, to accomplish whatever she sets out to do, to keep me grounded, to the best of her ability remind me of who I really am, who we are and what we share.

The story of trust from a man in one of our courses:

The first experience that developed my trust was when I first met Samuel, who feels like my soul brother. Samuel was doing bodywork with me in a session in which I was experiencing the birth struggle. He had amazed me by his total attention to each person he worked with, with his extraordinary selflessness. He stayed with me, his arms around me, and I thrashed and struggled and sweated and shouted for a long, long time. Finally there was a breakthrough from struggle to release, tenderness and vulnerability. I thought Samuel would want to get some relief from my sweat-soaked body, but I felt very needy. I asked, 'Can we just stay here for a little while?' He said, 'We can stay here as long as you want.' The generosity, love, devotion and selflessness of that overwhelmed me, because I knew he meant it. I burst into tears and sobbed as he held me. He stayed until I was completely ready for him to go.

We've known each other 12 years now. As I started working alongside him, my idealized image of him fell apart, only to give way to a deeper understanding of what an honest practitioner, what a true saint he is. Knowing his life so intimately, and how central his practice is in it, I can trust him, if he loses touch with his heart and our bond, to reconnect himself to his heart and me to mine. Also, because he is prepared to be so human, so un-saintly and flawed, I know there is no phony spirituality, no claim to anything really.

I've tested Samuel by giving other endeavors priority, by dropping out of contact for long periods. He never wavers in his respect and love for me. Even if we let each other down, the forgiveness is always going to be there. I think Samuel and I have been of one heart in our feeling about each other for a long time. Through Samuel, I think I can trust many people. Everyone is actually like Samuel! All flawed, all with a divine heart, traveling as best they can. I don't consciously try to see it in everyone, and so forget this to some degree. But I can see it when I focus.

Reflections on Step Three

In Step One, you made a commitment. You've explored the ways that past commitments have formed milestones on your path through life, and how your path has had ups and downs that together create forward motion. You've seen that a commitment is a leap into the unknown, propelled by an aspiration within yourself. Your commitments carry out the intention that formed you as an individual out of the fabric of the universe. The willful determination of each individual moves the whole cosmos in some direction; by your commitments you direct the process of creation.

Each of your commitments focuses your precious attention. One does, indeed, *pay* attention; attention 'capital,' which is limited, is paid to each commitment. The commitments you have discarded, as well as the commitments you have confirmed, have been the left and right steps of your path.

In Step Two, you saw how the process of testing demonstrates your real priorities and proves to yourself which friends, which interests, and which aspects of yourself are genuine. The tests you perform, you perform on behalf of the universe; the tests you receive are the actions of the universe probing its own mind and verifying its course. Step Two is a surrender in the sense that you are bound by your commitments, which determine how your time and energy are allocated.

Now in Step Three, you break through the testing and recommitting cycle to the clarity of knowledge, competency and trust. Testing is over for many steps of the path. (A more severe test occurs much later, in Step 8.) In reaching Step Three, you have reached a point of being able to easily trust, harmonize with and know a person or a situation. Your intentions have proven to be sincere, so they are quickly adopted by the universe without a test.

> Consider, is there someone you feel you can trust completely, due to your long association or the depth of your bonding (testing)? How is harmony and trust shown in your relationship? How did you get to this step beyond testing with this person?

Rick Bailey
Met early 90's
Became my Clinical Supervisor
Maintained relat. thru every other week to date.

Chapter 12
Step 4: Idealization

There are people who look at life with their brain, or their head as they call it, and there are others who look at life with their heart. And between these two points of view there is a vast difference; so much difference that something that one sees on the earth the other sees in heaven, something that one sees as small the other sees as great, something that one sees as limited the other sees as unlimited. These two types of people become opposite poles.[28]

Moving from Mind-Centered to Heart-Centered

STEP FOUR IS A GREAT BREAKTHROUGH in realization that changes your center of identity from your head to your heart. In our travels we often hear people say, "I wish I could get out of my head and drop down into my heart." But the feeling of the heart is the most natural thing; how could anyone be deprived of it? Why do so many people rely only upon their minds when the insight and courage of the heart is so readily available? Because in order to use your heart you have to feel your heart, and for many people, their heart feels sore, so they cover it. People generally at-

[28] Hazrat Inayat Khan, Vol. 8, Sufi Teachings, The Heart Quality, Looking at Life from the Heart

tribute their heart pain to what others have done to them, but it is the nature of the sensitive heart to feel pain and every heart has been wounded. The difference between people is not that one's been hurt and another not, but that one has healed their pain and the other not. If resentment, regret or fear accumulates in your heart, it becomes a poison that corrodes your heart and makes it inoperable. Consider this teaching from Hazrat Inayat Khan on the heart:

> There is a story told in Arabia that the angels descended from Heaven to earth and cut open the breast of the Prophet; they took away something that was to be removed from there, and then the breast was made as before. It is a symbolical expression, which gives to a key to the secret of human Life.
>
> What closes the doors of the heart is fear, confusion, depression, spite, discouragement, disappointment, and a troubled conscience; and when that is cleared away, the doors of the heart open.
>
> The opening of the breast, really speaking, is the opening of the heart. The sensation of joy is felt in the center of the breast, also the heaviness caused by depression. Therefore as long as the breast remains choked with anything, the heart remains closed. When the breast is cleared from it, the heart is open.
>
> It is the open heart which takes the reflection of all impressions coming from outside. It is the open heart which can receive reflections from the Divine Spirit within. It is the openness of heart, again, which gives power and beauty to express oneself; and if it is closed, a person, however learned, cannot express his or her learning to others.
>
> This symbolical legend explains also what is necessary to allow the plant of divine love to grow in one's heart –

remove that element which gives the bitter feeling. Just as there is a poison in the sting of the scorpion, and as there is a poison in the teeth of the snake, so there is poison in the heart, which is made to be the shrine of God. But God cannot arise in the shrine which is as dead by its own poison; it must be purified first, and made real, for God to arise. The heart [of the prophet] who had to sympathize with the whole world was thus prepared, that the drop of that poison which always produces contempt, resentment, and ill feeling against another, was destroyed first.

So many talk about the purification of heart, and so few really know what it is. Some say to be pure means to be free from all evil thought of bitterness against another. No one with sense and understanding would like to keep a drop of poison in their body, and how ignorant it is when anyone keeps and cherishes a bitter thought against another in their heart. If a drop of poison can cause the death of the body, it is equal to a thousand deaths when the heart retains the smallest thought of bitterness.

In this legend the cutting open of the breast is the cutting open of the shell over the heart. And the taking away of that element is that every kind of thought or feeling against anyone in the world has been taken away, and the breast, which means the heart, is filled with love alone, which is the real life of God. – HIK[29]

It is the opening of your heart that turns the whole world from black-and-white to technicolor. To open, your heart must be healed, or the pain your heart has will be too

[29] Hazrat Inayat Khan, Vol. 9, The Unity of Religious Ideals, The Symbology of Religious Ideas, the Opening of the Breast of the Prophet

much and you will close your heart and fall back upon the limited resource of your mind. How your heart can be healed is the topic of another book, but in brief, it cannot be done by avoiding the wound, nor by dwelling upon it. You must come to appreciate your wound, not regret it, and this will result from a change in energy, not a change in thinking.

No doubt you have experienced an opening of your heart at some time, for some period. If it lasted long enough to change your approach and direct your behavior, then you have really benefited. The attainment of Step Four is the ability to see from your heart the beauty in all hearts, even when people are unaware, inconsiderate or hurtful.

Some people live a long time before taking this step. Some people get it in childhood and never lose it. This step is not age-related—it can occur at any moment, and that moment will change you forever. Step Four will fill you with longing, aspiration, joy without reason, and an inconsolable longing. This is a living heart!

Step 4 in the Labyrinth

So far, the path has been easy to understand; we have been walking the steps of the mind. In the labyrinth, the path has been almost linear, with one excursion in Step Two. The path from here on gets more and more complex: sometimes progress is made by going backwards, while forward-heading paths may lead away from the goal. To the mind it's all very confusing; the mind likes straight lines and consistency but the heart enjoys circular movements, like stirring. Until now, you could observe yourself objectively and clearly; now it's going to get complicated, involved and subjective, like falling in love. Rules are going out the window; you're ruled by something else now, something that has grabbed your heart.

The breakthrough of Step Four is dramatic; you no doubt remember when it occurred. It is the brightest, most profound and memorable moment in a sea of forgettable years. This breakthrough is the opening of your heart. It occurs not just once, but again and again, in different areas of life. It might occur first in a religious setting, or in art, or in love making, or in school, anywhere. Later it will occur in a different arena. Eventually it can be invoked anytime, anywhere, at will.

This breakthrough is symbolized by the labyrinth's path suddenly moving from the left side of the circle to the right side. From the "3" in this diagram, the path descends and whips back and forth on the left side, representing the mind, until the mind is cleansed and prepared anew. Then the path springs to the right side, representing the heart. This is the first time that the path has entered the right side of the labyrinth, opening up a new world of possibilities.

You remember the symptoms of the opening of your heart:

- It came suddenly, surprisingly, unexpectedly.
- You couldn't speak or process thoughts normally.
- Time stopped.
- You can remember the moment like it was yesterday.
- It was an intensely emotional experience, and recalling it is still emotional.
- There was a sense of magic to it, and tremendous importance.

- You saw, heard, and felt sensations you never had before.
- It may have been life-changing, ushering in a new chapter of your life.

You've had this experience at least once, and you'll have it again.

- Some people try to deny the significance of this opening. They prefer a world that is asleep, mechanical and predictable. The excitement fades and they forget about the most important vision of their lives, when they saw life through their heart. They will go back to the sleep of reason.
- Some people are disturbed by the opening. They become frightened by the reality that is bigger and more alive than they had ever guessed. They can not imagine how they could control such a complex and interconnected world. They flee back to the safety of what they understand and fear others who are attracted to anything beyond that.
- Some people are despondent after the opening has come and gone. Having had a glimpse of heaven, they want another, desperately. The old life has no attraction for them anymore. The old objectives are meaningless. Life has new goals now as one aspires to the ideal of one's soul.

The opening has been described by many teachers, usually associated with "consciousness." Clearly, consciousness has changed dramatically. But what caused the change? *The opening of the heart is the cause; the awakening of consciousness is the effect.* It is the energy of the heart that awakens the mind from its slumber.

Concentration - Contemplation

The first three steps developed the mind, giving the ability to observe objectively and gain knowledge. The next three steps develop the heart, giving the ability to become what you see. Hazrat Inayat Khan calls the former skill **Concentration**, and the latter skill, **Contemplation**. The difference is in the point-of-view. As long as you maintain your own identity, you are observing. When you identify with something or someone else, then you are contemplating.[30]

Saint Francis entered a period of contemplation when he was walking through the forest one day and suddenly thought, "The trees are looking at me." He was no longer identified with himself; he was identified with the trees and he experienced what they experienced in seeing a person walking among them.

Contemplation can occur in everyday life, and when it does, it gives a new way of seeing that can solve problems you couldn't solve with your old way of seeing. Puran reports:

> *I was having a problem with a computer program that I was attempting to run on a new, experimental computer. There were no debugging aids, external devices that reveal what the computer is doing internally, and by observation of the computer's outputs I could not tell where it was stopping. I concentrated intensely on the program I had written, but I didn't see where I had gone wrong. So I contemplated the computer: I started by staring at its metal and silicon body. Then I breathed in the computer, into my heart. I felt the computer*

[30] For a longer discussion of Concentration, Contemplation, and Meditation, see *Living from the Heart*, pp 34-53

and then I felt like *the computer. I had the body of the computer and I had the mind of the computer. Instantly I got a feeling of looping. I examined my feelings and found where the looping was occurring. That led me directly to the erroneous code. I might have found this error eventually by concentration alone, but contemplation proved to be a shortcut.*

It is the deeper part of mind that is used in contemplation; this deeper part of the mind we call "heart." The surface of the heart we call "mind."

In Heart Rhythm Meditation, you mastered concentration on your heart; you could feel and sustain the sensation of heartbeat in your chest. This sensation was the proof that your focus was really on your heart. You were not just thinking about your heart, you were actually concentrating very intensely to experience that, "My heart is inside me."

In Step Four, you actually experience that *"I am inside my heart,"* as your heart becomes an enormous room. You see yourself from the point-of-view of your heart instead of seeing your heart from the point-of-view of your eyes. Stage Two, starting with Step Four, allows you to experience the contemplation of your heart, in which you go inside your heart and take its identity. This is the switch in identity that distinguishes contemplation from concentration.

You can also feel the condition of another's heart as if it is your own. Until this step, the contemplation of another is largely fantasy. It is the idealization of your heart that allows you to see deeply into another. One can see and understand only as much as one can respect and love. Idealization allows you to recognize your ideal in any person, which then gives you access to their heart.

Seeing from the Heart

What the mind sees is what it can *understand*. There are many cases of scientists overlooking a discovery because they could not imagine it. It was right in front of them but they were not able to understand what they saw, so they saw what they understood. A simple example is the sight of a sunrise. Unless you can understand that the sun is the center of the earth's orbit you cannot see that the sun does not rise; the Earth bows.

What the heart sees is what it *remembers*. The heart is deeply impressed by the memory of the soul's experience in the worlds of unending light and unconditional love. The mind is connected to the senses; the heart has only indirect access to them, through the mind. But a single note of music that reaches the heart can set it to ecstasy in the memory of celestial vibrations. A simple color or form can so move the heart in its memory of light and beauty that it sighs, weeps, jumps or responds with a brilliant creativity.

People who have not made this step tend to think that an idealist is unrealistic and romantic. But you are now aware of a greater portion of reality than the obvious surface that appears to everyone. You are seeing what is developing from the inside of things, what *can* be because it already *is*.

The heart gives off light when it's energized. (This is measurable with a photon counter.[31]) Illumined by this light, the world looks like a different place; it begins to look like heaven.

---

[31] Puran participated in an interesting experiment which demonstrates the heart's luminescence. Bair (2007).

- The mundane, flat, black-and-white world is revealed before the eyes of the heart to be extraordinary, deep and colorful.
- You are filled with the heart's natural experience of deep connection with and profound appreciation for everything.
- Surprised by the possibilities, you can see what could be instead of what is.
- Then you see what IS instead of what appears.
- The outer forms of things open to your open heart and their inner forms are revealed.
- Now you discover the external world to be a mirror of your internal self.
- You begin to glimpse a grand purpose in your life.

The discovery of the ideal is a breakthrough caused by an opening of your heart. At Step Four you can see the ideal in others because you have discovered an ideal inside yourself. What you have found inside, you can see outside in others, but you can only see in yourself what you have seen first in someone else, a teacher, for example.

This step can also be called "The Discovery of the Soul," where soul means the pure, essential being, the seed of divine nature. In heart meditation, you can see your soul reflected in the depth of your heart. This is what awakens your sense of ideal, which is so central to this step on the path that we call Step Four, "Idealization."

The Ideal

> In this fourth step there is the ideal of your imagination.
> – HIK[32]

> All the beautiful forms that exist are forms of this ideal, all the good qualities that one finds in a person belong to this ideal, and also all the different ways of expressing one's respect and devotion that one sees in the world. And in this way, as one progresses through life, one makes the ideal better and better, greater and greater, higher and higher, till the ideal is perfect.
> – HIK[33]

Your sense of ideal comes from your heart; your sense of what is practical comes from your mind. Naturally, your ideal is much greater than what you think is practical, because your heart is much greater than your mind. And also, it is natural that the practical person should ridicule the idealist, because the mind cannot imagine what the heart knows to be true.

What is your ideal? For every person, the ideal is different because your ideal originates in your soul, and your soul is unique. The ideal of your soul is your vision of the purpose of your life. Your ideal colors the pure, white light of spirit and fills your heart with colored light. When your heart is open, this light radiates to fill your mind and body, and then outward into your life. But if your heart is closed, your ideal cannot express itself, and this is a cause of spiritual discontent.

To get a clue about what your ideal is, consider this

---

[32] Hazrat Inayat Khan, Vol. 10, The Path of Initiation and Discipleship, 1. The Path of Initiation

[33] Hazrat Inayat Khan, Vol. 11, Mysticism in Life, 6. The Ideal of the Mystic

question: "What is it that the world needs most right now?" Everyone has a different answer to this question, once you dig deeper than the superficial answers like "world peace," and your answer gives a powerful clue to the ideal of your soul, as felt by your heart and expressed by your mind.

Take some time and consider this carefully, in a meditation. "What is it that the world needs most right now?" Journal your answer to record it, and then consider the following question...

If that's what you think is *most important*, why aren't you devoting to it every moment of your life and every resource you have? Your inability and unwillingness to do so is a second cause of spiritual discontent, and it accompanies the spiritual buoyancy and joy of discovering your ideal to begin with.

There is a third source of spiritual discontent that arises with the ideal—the realization that every person's ideal is different. You need to nurture and strengthen your own ideal, while allowing others the same. This may increase conflicts between people. For example, this story from Puran:

> *After I became a draft resister during the Vietnam War, I had the opportunity to meet and talk with the man in charge of the military draft in the U.S., General Lewis Hershey. He said he understood that my ideal was peace, but his ideal was national security, and he didn't think it was just and fair to let my ideal encroach upon his. I tried to argue that my ideal was greater than his ideal, but such arguments cannot be resolved.*

A disagreement about ideals is at the heart of every argument. For example, the debate about whether abortion should be legal is a conflict between the two distinct ideals of the sacredness of an unborn child versus the freedom of a woman to make choices about her own body.

These few examples have mentioned some ideals: peace, security, sacredness, and freedom. Some other common ideals are power, knowledge, affiliation, beauty, kindness, compassion, trustworthiness, dependability, responsibility, justice, loyalty, and truth. There are many more, as many as there are colors in the rainbow and souls on the earth. Your ideal cannot be reasoned away or dismissed; it is defined in your soul.

If you seek power, you will aspire to positions of power and you will seek friends and lovers who can teach you about power and/or help you be powerful. You will come to understand power in people, you will be drawn to power in nature, in business, sports and politics. Ultimately, you will make an idol of power and devote yourself to it.

> *Peter always said that he married Judy for her incredible beauty, and indeed she had that quality strongly. But he came to realize that he actually married her for her devotion to him, which helped him become more successful and powerful. This became clear when she began to pursue her own development instead of serving him. Judy was not less beautiful, but still she was less desirable to Peter because his ideal was not beauty, but power.*

If you seek beauty, you will sacrifice power for it. You will sacrifice comfort for it. An artist we know was content to have very little as long as he had a violin. Then he desired other forms of beauty beside music, and spent his money on acquiring some beautiful objects. His favorite place to visit was not the beach or a mountain cabin, but the museum of art. He loved to be around beautiful people, and he could appreciate the beauty in most anyone. Beauty was his sole ideal; he couldn't get enough beauty because beauty fed his soul.

When your heart opens and your idealism is piqued, your life will not be content for a long time. Pursuit of your ideal will drive your life's decisions and allocate your time and resources. Most importantly, your pursuit of your ideal is the surest way to discover yourself, for your concept of ideal is a vision of your own nature.

The Ideal in Relationships

The opening of the heart offers a much deeper level of intimacy, vulnerability and empathy than was possible in Step Three. The ideal that the heart reveals is surprising, and both comforting and irritating:

- It is surprising because it occurs after you think you've understood, and suddenly you see in a person, a situation, and a path, the qualities of the divine. You see the traces of your ideal—that which is perfect, eternal and infinite—in people and things and you are transformed by what you see. People who have not made this step assume that an idealist is unrealistic and romantic. But you know you are aware of a greater portion of reality than the obvious surface that appears to everyone. You are seeing what is developing from the inside of things, what can be because it already is.
- It is comforting because you know immediately you have seen the self you have always searched for. Until now, life has been one frantic search for the self—through trying to find the perfect pair of shoes that is "me," the car that best expresses "me," the job that brings out "me," the relationship where "I can be me," etc. Now you realize you've found it: the essen-

tial and eternal "me." Your life will never be the same. You now have real insight into who you are because you've discovered qualities of your real self. And you see those qualities of yourself in others, in nature, in situations, and in ordinary things. You have been awakened. You see in all things the potential to become your ideal.

- It is irritating because people can't seem to maintain the qualities you can see in them. They can't live the way they really are. Also, the stakes of the game of life are raised. Life is no longer about pleasure, or understanding, or success in the usual terms. The ideal has appeared, and now nothing else can be as important. Although your ideal has been envisioned, it is not grasped, and consequently you will experience discontent. You can see it, but you can't *be* it. (This will be solved by Step Five.)

The ideal you discover and see in others is uniquely your own ideal, as it reflects the qualities of your own soul. Although you can see this ideal in others, no one can completely live up to it because it is *your* ideal, which you create from your insight into your soul and memories you have of infinite beauty, pure light and unconditional love. Other people have their own, different ideal to which they aspire. Still, you can see the ideal of your heart reflected in the hearts of others and that makes others incredibly attractive.

Step Four allows love to develop from passion to adoration, from a selfish "high" to an unselfish devotion. When your heart opens and your whole world changes, whoever is with you and wherever you are at that time will be important to you from then on. If you have an opening of your heart in nature, you will be drawn to nature for the rest of your life. If your heart opening occurs in church, you will return again and again to try to re-experience the feeling you had there. If your heart opens in the presence of a person, you will love that person without bounds.

Morality

The mind is built to engage and process the senses. It has been tuned to make fine discriminations between colors, sounds, flavors and sensations. By the fabulous ability of the mind, we can recognize different people by slight variations in their appearance or voice, a very useful skill. All that the mind perceives it considers to be outside and other than itself, for objectivity. This leads us to think that other people are quite distinct and separate from ourselves.

For people whose experience of life is dominated by their minds, real compassion is not possible. If you see someone else as disconnected from yourself, then why should you care what they feel? The highest morality that a mind-centered person can aspire to is the Biblical Golden Rule:

Do unto others what you would have them do unto you. [34]

The Golden Rule was created to meet people where they are, which is mostly in the mind. In so doing, it makes human relationships into a kind of business deal: "I'll do this for you so that you will do the same for me." There's no heart in that; it's just intelligent self-interest.

With the opening of the heart, a sense of connection between yourself and all others becomes undeniable. The Golden Rule is no longer your ideal of morality. With the

---

[34] Matthew 7:12, Luke 6:31

discovery of your heart it now makes sense to be generous. Your every kindness to another will come back to you like an echo in a canyon or a reflection in a mirror. Every thought, word, and deed will reverberate in your life.

The kinds of statements made elsewhere in the Bible, such as *love thy neighbor as thyself*, or *love your enemies, do good to those who hate you,*[35] begin to make a new kind of sense. If someone asks you to walk a mile with them, you continue for two miles. If they ask for your coat, you give your shirt also.[36] You cannot be exploited and you cannot be victimized because you give from love, willingly.

- Whatever you give to anyone will echo in your life.
- Whatever you receive you must return in some form to someone, sooner or later.
- If another person gives you something, they receive a blessing greater than what you gained.
- If another person takes something from you, you will be given in other ways more than you lost.

This morality is not "reasonable." It cannot be argued. If your heart is not open, no one can convince you of these things. If your heart is open, no one can convince you otherwise.

On Initiation

Each of the steps in realization is such a significant event that they are referred to in a spiritual school as "initiations." This is the first step and the first initiation. By recognizing the step as an initiation, you are acknowledging that some-

---

[35] Luke 10:27, Luke 6:27

[36] Matthew 5:40-41

thing has happened that will become a milestone in your life, a permanent change of state. Having realized the value of commitment, you will be able to meet future challenges as opportunities for engagement.

Here is the explanation of Hazrat Inayat Khan on initiation:

> Initiation is like the experience of a person who has never learnt how to swim, who steps into the river or into the sea for the first time, without knowing, "Will I be able to float or will I be swept away and drowned?"
>
> *Every person has had an initiation in the worldly sense in some form or other*. When a business person begins an entirely new enterprise, and there is no support at this moment except the thought, "No matter whether I lose or gain, I will take a step forward, I will go into this enterprise although I do not know what will happen later," then that person undergoes a worldly initiation. And the first attempt of someone who wants to learn to ride, if they have never been on horseback before nor driven a horse, so that they do not know where the horse will take them—this also is an initiation.
>
> But initiation in the real sense of the word, as it is used on the spiritual path, takes place when a person, in spite of having a religion and belief, an opinion and ideas about spiritual things, feels that they should take a step in a direction which they do not know; when they take the first step, that is an initiation.
>
> Ghazali, a great Sufi writer of Persia, has said that *entering the spiritual path is just like shooting an arrow at a point one cannot see*, so that one does not know what the arrow is going to hit; one only knows one's own action, and one does not see the point aimed at. This is why the path of initiation is difficult for a worldly person. Human na-

> ture is such that one born into this world, who has become acquainted with the life of names and forms, wants to know everything by name and form, to touch something in order to be sure that it exists. Therefore it is difficult to undergo an initiation on a path which does not touch any of the senses. One does not know where one is going.[37]

The term "initiation" signifies these steps on the path as highly consequential, permanent transitions. Sometimes the stress of an initiation exceeds a person's capacity, and illness, depression or addiction follows for some time. When an initiation is consciously affirmed by a teacher who knows The Map of milestones on the path of human development, the after-shocks of an initiation are more easily handled. The even-numbered initiations are generally more difficult to assimilate.

Step 4 in the Spiritual School

> In this fourth initiation there is this ideal of man's imagination. Once this initiation is received a person begins to radiate, to radiate his ideal which is within him as his initiator. —HIK[38]

The opening of your heart in this step allows you to see your ideal in a human being. You might have taken a teacher before this step, but your mind wouldn't have been able to appreciate the depth of love in your teacher until this step of the heart is attained.

There is a practice called *Tasawwuri,* which means to think of your teacher as the focus of your ideal. In this fourth

---

[37] Hazrat Inayat Khan, *Volume 10, The Path of Initiation and Discipleship*. 1. The Path of Initiation, A Step Forward.
[38] *Ibid.,* 1. The Path of Initiation, 4th Initiation.

step you begin this practice, a most beneficial form of the practice of Contemplation. At this step, your teacher is a person you know, who knows you; at a later step it is the Christ or Prophet (called *Rasul*); still later it is God.

> The thought of the teacher is not given only that a student may concentrate on a form from which to seek inspiration, but also that the student may keep before himself or herself an ideal, not only to look up to but to come up to. And this can be done by trying every moment of one's life to think as the teacher thinks, to see as the teacher sees, to feel as the teacher feels, and to act as the teacher acts in different situations. This means a perfect self-effacement, which makes the soul a mirror. The teacher, reflected in that mirror, becomes the spirit of the mirror, and therefore one becomes the same spirit which one holds in one's soul. —Hazrat Inayat Khan

The Peaks and the Base

The steps of the path are like the game of "Chutes and Ladders." You go along a linear path, then come to a ladder that takes you to a whole new level. But a few steps later you may fall into a chute that instantly transports you back even farther than you were. When we have a moment of an opening, it's a peak experience that may last for some minutes, hours or even a few days. Then we fall back to a base level. (In Sufi literature, you will find the peak experience referred to as a *Hal* while the base state is called the *Maqqum.*)

Many peak experiences eventually accumulate to raise the level of the base. Each peak adds confidence and leaves a trail of energy that is widened and deepened with repetition. It's like hiking in the woods where initially there is no trail—if you want to revisit the destination, you will remember the way vaguely. The next time you will go more quickly, and every time the path will get easier until it's paved over like a highway.

A peak experience is like being a guest; the base place is what you own and call home. Your base is a home state you can go to at will; to be a guest at the peak resort is a gift.

This explains why we can have a life-changing peak experience and then fall back to our old condition. All the old, immature, undeveloped behaviors are still available to us. We are always animals and angels, and it is no trick to act like an animal, so we do sometimes. But our attainment of Step Four is shown by the ability to shake ourselves and quickly return home to the place of the heart, in any circumstance.

If you don't have the key and you have to wait to be invited in, then you can't say you live there. But if you have a good example to aspire to and a good practice to depend on, you can eventually claim the most beautiful palace as your rightful inheritance. Yesterday's peak experience (Hal) will become tomorrow's base experience (Maqqum).

What Awakening Feels Like

Puran describes a moment of awakening he experienced:

In 1983 I met my wife, Susanna. She was standing against a wall with a group of people standing around her, talking. I was leaving the hall where my teacher had been speaking and I suddenly stopped to look at her, stunned. A friend who was walking beside me started to pull on me, asking, "Why are you looking at her? Who is she?"

"I don't know," I answered. "There is something about her... like I remember her." I don't remember anything else about that day – not even what my teacher had spoken about. In that

moment my heart opened and I could remember a being I had known before. It would take four years for Susanna and I to be together. There were many obstacles in the way, but I jumped them because I had an ideal. The path from this moment to our eventual marriage was practically impossible and turned out to be very painful for me and many others. I was not proceeding rationally; I was crazy in love.

Not all love is crazy; many loving partnerships arise from mutual needs, common interests, practical benefits, years of history together, or convenience. Our relationship developed those things later, but it started from an awakening moment. My heart opened and allowed me to experience a memory in my soul that gave rise to an ideal, which I then pursued.

Here is a story from one of our students:

I hated everything about where I was and who I was with. It was all so fake and derelict. I left them and walked along a very busy highway for a few hours, diving into despair. There seemed no purpose or beauty in life at all. I was as low as I could go. I remember standing on a bridge looking down at the traffic, thinking, "There is no point in any of it. We're born, we eat, we procreate and we die. I would kill myself but what is the point? I would just be born again and have to go through it all in another form." I was so depressed that even suicide didn't seem to offer release.

I walked on and on in abject despair. Then, in the space of an instant, it felt as if the earth itself overrode my circuitry. I came over the crest of a hill to a beautiful vista of the afternoon sunlight hitting a broad river. And it felt as if the light from the earth and the sky entered me and cleansed me as a wave of pure energy. I was overwhelmed with the knowledge that this body was a sacred gift, this life one of infinite potential. And the excitement in the responsibility of serving this sacred energy as truly as possible was immense. I realized in that moment the darkness and the light, and the profound lov-

ing duty we all have to choose well for ourselves and all beings. The change this led to wasn't instant on all levels, yet it has been inexorable. I never knew before that it was a choice, almost a blessed obligation, to cultivate that power that we all have in us in different forms.

An awakening can be the witnessing of an injustice, as was the case with one of the mentors and teachers in our school, Elizabeth Smith:

My elementary school was desegregated when I was in the sixth grade. On the way home one day, I passed the high school and wandered into the gym. I have a very strong, clear memory of the smell of sweat and urine. When I got inside, I saw that two young black men had been tied to the basketball goals. One had urinated on himself. There were several white males underneath both of the young black men. They had their belts out and they were hitting the black boys, not very hard. The white boys were laughing and making jokes. The air of humiliation was thick; none of the adults in the room was intervening, although some seemed upset. Two white police officers stood around doing nothing.

In remembering this, I feel the same way I did then: frozen, like I want to throw up, disappear. I see the episode from up high, outside of my body, and at the same time from down low, feeling sick to my stomach about the human race. I feel powerless and completely overcome with anger. My world goes quiet. My ears turn off. There is no thinking, just feeling. I walk out in shock.

This day brought a feeling of overwhelming hope—I had seen a long stream of black children with their parents coming to school that morning, dressed in their Sunday best, and it had been so beautiful I'd had to hold back tears—and then came this feeling of dark despair and anger.

Such realizations can seem utterly paradoxical—a recognition that humanity is capable of both intolerable cruelty and incredible generosity. Paula Roome wrote of her moment of awakening:

> *I was brokenhearted. I could not stop crying. My feelings of desperation for the world, how we as humans treat each other, our cruelty, the wars we inflict, our greed... they overwhelmed me. Then I saw our beauty, our capacities for hope and love, our willingness to try to make a difference, the openness of people's hearts.*

Others have experiences of synchronicity—which, when they happen consistently, are a sign of Step 4. They reveal the heart's effect on the mind. The mind just cannot comprehend the complexity of the interconnectedness of life's events; it cannot sense the forces at work, tugging on the strings that operate the universe, but has to recognize those forces when they emerge through synchronicity. Here's a story that provides a good example of this:

> *I was walking down the road with a friend, in a state of exultation. We were talking about someone who was troubled. I said I saw her as an exotic, wounded bird, and a few steps later we came across a brilliantly colored dying bird on the road.*
>
> *On the way home I bought a cappuccino in the airport. When the guy handed it to me, I saw that he had made a beautiful swirling pattern in the froth: a wonderful heart of many layers. We were bowled over by this sign that we were on the Path of the Heart.*

The heart is actually the creative fount of such forces. Synchronistic events are the breaking-through of the heart into the space of the mind.

In the Aftermath of Awakening Experience

Some people try to deny the significance of this awakening as soon as it happens. This urge can be so powerful that the awakening moment is forgotten. If you carry that awakening forward with you and integrate it into your life, you can't go back into a world that is mechanical, predictable, asleep—the kind of world that is the preferred place of residence for those who fear mystical experience.

It is not surprising that some people are disturbed by awakening, even when that awakening is joyful. The reality they glimpse is bigger and more alive than they had ever guessed. They cannot imagine how they could control such a complex and interconnected world. Control (or, as is the case, the *illusion* of control) is still important to them, and so they flee back to the safety of what they understand. Once the excitement fades, it is easy to forget about having glimpsed a vision of life lived through the heart and to go back to the sleep of reason.

Some people fall into despondency after the awakening has come and gone. Having had a glimpse of heaven, they want another, desperately. The old life has no attraction for them anymore. The old objectives are meaningless. Life has new goals now as one aspires to the ideal of one's soul.

The Difficult Aspects of Idealization

As is the case with any major shift, Step 4 has its challenges; as it is an even-numbered step, its challenge involves surrender. Step 4 involves a much deeper surrender than what had occurred during your testing in Step 2. It is a surrender of personal aspirations to your newly discovered ideal.

The discovery of the ideal can feel like a rude surprise. It occurs after your mind has come to believe that you've understood pretty much all that requires understanding. And then, suddenly, you see—in a person, a situation, a path—qualities of the divine. You see traces of the ideal: flashes of perfection, eternity, and infinity appear in people and things. These insights are transformative; perhaps at first you think it's merely imagination or fantasy, a case of seeing what you want to see. But in time you see that this way of looking at the world is both real and more compelling than your old paradigm. A whole new way of seeing, experiencing, and being begins to emerge, and it can feel like you're starting all over again.

Despite the great aspects of awakening that we've described so far, attaining Step Four will likely make your life much harder. Holding an ideal makes life far more difficult. As your heart awakens, your mind suddenly realizes it has been superseded by a much more powerful faculty; your mind is simply not capable of the vision and the power of the heart. This realization can be quite upsetting. You see that while the world and the beings in it are more wonderful than you ever imagined, you're not going to be able to use your mind, which you've trusted and depended upon your whole life, to experience this wonder. Not knowing the ways of the heart yet, you have to wait for these marvelous life-changing moments to happen, like a light coming on in a dark room. Before you were used to the darkness, and now you know there is much more, and indeed, that darkness is not your natural state.

Moments of awakening are fleeting, and in between, you find you cannot hold the beauty of your awakening, so you slip back into your previous mental paradigm, which is comforting, yet unsatisfying.

One student described his frustration with seeking out

awakening experiences:

> *I push as hard into it as I can and nothing happens. Then, I wait—quit, really—and then something happens.*

The pushing is important—this is concentration that focuses your attention—but it isn't enough. Awakening into the heart also requires intention. With these two pieces in place, the process begins that evolves from deep, intense concentration into a more passive period where the fruit of the effort can be realized. It is a process much like the growth of a fruit: the plant marshals an enormous amount of energy to produce the fruit before it ever appears. Allowing yourself to go into a passive state where you are utterly open and vulnerable requires an enormous trust that whatever happens will be right. For the person who likes to feel capable and in control, this can be a huge challenge.

Using Drugs for Awakening

Many people have described awakenings they experienced while under the influence of drugs. As the noted spiritual teacher and author Ram Dass used to say, drug experiences can be useful because they show us an alternate reality—but they only allow us to visit; we can't stay. We would say that the experience on drugs is not more realistic, it is actually delusional. What you experience in meditation is different; why can we say it is more realistic? Because it is operable; you can actually change physical reality with meditation.

Puran had a clear view of this when he met Timothy Leary, who was a great proponent of psychedelic drugs as a vehicle for personal development and spiritual awakening.

> *In 1980, when Timothy Leary came to my home, he was barely articulate. He spoke in long sentences with big words that*

made no sense. I didn't bother to challenge him. There was no point; I just felt sorry for him. He bore the cost of being a pioneer. No one knew, back then, the long-term effects of LSD. Ram Dass had been a close friend and collaborator with Leary in the early days of experimentation with psychedelic drugs, but as he moved deeper into his spiritual practice, he abandoned the use of drugs as a method of awakening.

The universe protects us; we do not see more of reality than we have the capacity to process. Drugs override this protective mechanism, which is why moments of awakening that are induced by drugs can be very difficult to integrate psychologically.

Any experience can be helpful or dangerous, depending upon what you bring to it, how strong your nervous system is, and how you interpret it afterward. Clearly, many people would never have been attracted to spirituality were it not for their experiences with drugs. Once you learn to meditate, however, any mind-altering substance will impose a ceiling on your meditations.

Drugs don't give you the energy you need to awaken; they borrow the energy. Repeated use of drugs often precipitates a depressive state as the drug draws energy from the cells of the body to deliver it to the heart. Either before or after the high, you will have a corresponding low. If you're lucky, the low occurs during sleep or a low-energy state that spreads across several days.

Our teacher forbade his students to use any drugs. Our way is not to forbid anything, for all experiences have value, and everyone must find the path as they can. We do not advise our students to use drugs to attain awakening experiences, simply because there are more reliable methods that do not carry the risks of delusion and the energetic drain.

We have found Heart Rhythm Meditation to be the single most effective way of awakening to the ideal within.

Reflection on Step Four

> Recall a moment of awakening you remember and how it changed your life. Perhaps the change didn't come immediately, but it was inexorable.
>
> Earlier, you examined how your commitments have initiated the chapters of your life. Now we want to look at how awakening has shaped your commitments.

An experience of awakening often is the starting point of a new commitment, but most commitments are made without such an awakening because moments of awakening are relatively rare. People mostly make a commitment because there's a good reason to do it, it makes sense and feels right. For example, many people marry without a heart-felt experience of falling in love. They spend a lot of time together, they are comfortable and accepting of one another, and they feel it's their duty to step into marriage as the next point of evolution of their relationship. They make a commitment of marriage that is based on trust and understanding (Step Three), but not the idealization that comes from the awakening of the heart in Step Four.

A marriage made in Step Three will be transformed by one person moving into Step Four; the relationship may be strained by one person's new challenges and passion that comes from discovering the ideal, or the relationship can enjoy a revival and renewal as the partners enter their own hearts and the hearts of the other.

When you have an amazing awakening experience that opens your heart, you can instantly make a commitment (Step One), without thinking. Then you have to go through

Testing (Step Two) and come to an understanding of what you've done (Step Three). But if you can hold the vision and emotion of the awakening, you can pass through those steps easily and quickly.

It is my way to have
my heart opened (step 1)
then be tested (step 2)
then come to an
understanding of what
I've done (Step three)
ex: Birth of son
ex: Marriage to [illegible]
ex: Care of Dave
ex: Agreeing to the
Bus/Gallery/Play
ex: Joining I AM-U
ex: Initiation

HOLD THE VISION + EMOTION

Chapter 13
Step 5: Expertise

> [Step 4] When we develop our sense of beauty, then we are naturally critical of that which does not come up to our standard. But when we have passed this stage, in the next cycle [Step 5] divine compassion is developed in our nature and we become able to add all that is lacking, and so to compensate for that perfect beauty. —HIK[39]

STEP FOUR BROUGHT AN AWAKENING of the heart, resulting in an amazing experience of the ideals of love, harmony and beauty of life. The challenge of Step Four's awakenings is to make commitments and priorities that carry out these exquisite insights and to go through the testing that makes sense of them. That requires you to understand with your mind what your heart already knows and is showing you through these moments of awakening. This is the challenge which we take up in Step Five.

Step Four had aspects that made you discontented and critical: you can see and feel the qualities of your soul, reflected in your heart, but you can't yet operate those qualities in your life. Your inability to behave in relationships in

---

[39] Hazrat Inayat Khan, Aphorisms

the way you now know is possible, or to accomplish something that would be worthy of your ideal, can bring frustration. *If only you could embody the understanding you hold in your heart…*

As long as your moments of awakening remain sparse, the periods in between can be more difficult than if you had never seen the possibility. Awakening appears first as an isolated, extraordinary moment in life, and following this moment, you might not have another such awakening for weeks, months, or years. But as you learn more about your heart, you will feel your heart springing open more often. For some, this particular difficulty never presents itself; the awakening of the heart comes early and often. *If only you could stay in that heart-centered space for longer periods, and more often…*

You can see the ideal in others, but they can't seem to live up to it either. *If only your partner, family and friends could be the way you see they could be…*

Another difficulty of Step 4 is that your heart is showing you a reality that many of the people around you deny—even trusted people like parents and friends This can bring feelings of isolation and cause an unwelcome shift in your relationships. You can see the ideal in life, but other people have other visions of a different ideal and argue with you; or they don't appreciate what you're seeing at all and dismiss you. *If only you could show them what you see…*

In Step Five, you experience a realization: no one else is going to bring your ideal to life. Indeed, the very reason you hold that particular ideal is to create it. This leads you to a breakthrough in power, where you develop the ability to create and convey the ideal you have seen.

The Creation of Your Ideal

In Step Five, your ideal shifts from an image to a living entity. You move from *imagining* the ideal into a state where your ideal resides *in you*. Your ideal becomes a sort of friend who walks with you through life—a friend who is always near and can always be counted upon.

You realize that although the conditions that will allow you to live the ideal of your heart cannot be found, these conditions can be created. This is a profound realization: your ideal will not be found in any place, situation, or person, but it can be created in any place, situation or person you choose. **Your ideal is not to be found, but made.**

Actually, it *must* be made. There's no other way to find it. Only *you* can construct your ideal, because your ideal is totally unique to you. In Step Five, you actually do it. You are no longer dependent on others to be the way you want them to be or to make a situation as you would like it. **You are the expert now, and you can construct your ideal.** You can paint it, sing it, write it down, build it up, and live in it.

In a relationship, you can bring out the ideal you see in another person. You have learned what you can do to develop in another what you see in them. At work, you create your own job and it is immensely satisfying to you. You have made your ideal real and it surrounds you; it is no longer conceptual or intangible. This gives you great satisfaction and a genuine self-confidence based on real ability.

Contemplation becomes operative

> It is difficult to explain to what extent the power of contemplation works; those who are acquainted with the working of contemplation can only call its result a phenomenon. The reason that the heart/mind is creative is

> because the divine spirit is creative, and because the divine spirit is creative therefore the heart/mind inherits, as its divine heritage, the faculty of creating. —HIK[40]

The fifth step is a great advance in the process of contemplation, the ability to switch identities with another person or thing. *Now you can communicate with that upon which you focus, and it guides you.* In Step Five, Contemplation is working in both directions, that is, you can understand the one you contemplate, and you can influence the one you contemplate. Whatever happens to one happens to the other. Through contemplation you can actually change that which you contemplate by bringing out inner qualities that are buried.

We call Step Five "Expertise." As an expert, you feel your success and your power; naturally, you want to be recognized by other experts in order to validate your own state. The expert knows well that his or her accomplishment has required a high degree of both personal mastery (to develop the ability to concentrate), and openness (to enter the state of contemplation). Expertise gives access to the most desirable people, who will accept you as their equal.

Step Five in Work

> One might ask to what extent contemplation can help. Nothing in the world is impossible for the contemplative person to accomplish if only (s)he knows how to contemplate. No doubt this is gibberish to those who do not understand the subject. People wonder what relation a person's heart has to affairs outside; perhaps one can heal oneself from illness, but if there is an affair outside

---

[40] Hazrat Inayat Khan, Vol. 12, The Vision of God and Man, The Path of Meditation

> which is going wrong, a money matter or a business transaction, what connection has that with the heart? The answer is that all that exists, whether it is business or anything else, all that is visible or invisible, seems to be outside, but in reality it is in our heart. It is outside because our eyes see it outside, but it is within us because the heart surrounds it. It is accommodated in our heart. Heart is an accommodation of the world which is outside.—HIK[41]

At work, you create your own job and it is immensely satisfying to you. Regardless of the job you were hired for, you have found your way to the critical position that is essential and that no one else can do. Your influence in the organization becomes enormous; even if you are not the most powerful by title, or the best paid, you are the one that performs the crucial function that makes everything work.

You have the glorious experience of being as great as you have ever imagined being. You're at the top of your game. You amaze yourself with all that you can understand, say and do. Recognition and admiration come from all sides.

Step Five in Relationships

The opening of your heart in Step Four allowed you to see the ideal in your partner, but also raised your expectations of him or her, leading to a more critical relationship. Idealism makes life more difficult because the ideal cannot be held—it can be glimpsed, which is incredibly attractive and compelling, but no one can live up to your ideal in life. Step Four, an even-numbered step, actually makes your relationship more fragile.

---

[41] Hazrat Inayat Khan, Vol. 4, Mental Purification, 12. Mystic Relaxation (2)

The attainment of Step Five is the solution that makes your relationship stable again. This is the realization that the way you relate to your partner has a huge effect upon their ability to stay in their heart. You know you can help your partner bring out their greatness and you know that people need help to see and become who they are. Because you recognize the many ways that your partner is great, you have a unique ability to guide their process of development and inspire them as you have been inspired, to open your heart.

> Is love pleasure, is love merriment? No, love is longing constantly; love is persevering unweariedly; love is hoping patiently; love is willing surrender; love is regarding constantly the pleasure and displeasure of the beloved, for love is resignation to the will of the possessor of one's heart; it is love that teaches one: "Thou, not I." — HIK[42]

When your partner is not being who you know they can be, you are not critical. Instead, you realize that, "I am not doing all that I could be doing to bring out the nobility, kindness, generosity, courage, harmony, joy, etc. of this person's heart." Since you've discovered the power of your heart, you're confident in your ability to influence and inspire your partner. In Step Five you see that it's your responsibility to create the ideal you seek and, since you see the ideal in your partner, your role is to serve him/her in becoming as great as you know him/her to be.

Step Five in Athletics

An athlete who is "in the zone" of exceptional performance is actually in a state of contemplation. To get into this zone, athletes are taught to pay keen attention to the basics

[42] Hazrat Inayat Khan, Gaya, Talas

of the game, concentrating on the steps, procedures, and exercises. Then, when concentration becomes very intense, he or she enters contemplation. Now the athlete is no longer aware of the steps and procedures that form the details of what he or she is doing; his or her behavior is automatic.[43] The focus is on the result, not the process, and the athlete's body automatically does what it must do to attain that result. An expert golfer, for example, does not focus on hitting the ball; he or she focuses on where the ball is going to go. The body takes care of the mechanics; the expert directs only the final result.

The specific skills of the sport are learned earlier, in concentration, a process that may take years, but excellence in the sport comes through *disregarding* the steps in an instantaneous switch of focus. At first the athlete performs the sport, now *the sport performs the athlete.* The coordination necessary for truly expert behavior is too complex for the mind; it must be done by the heart. When asked about how she does what she does, the athlete snaps out of the zone. Self-observation is the antithesis of contemplation.

You can see when an athlete cannot maintain the state of contemplation, and switches back to concentration, for it is accompanied by a complete breakdown in performance. It's called *choking,* and it sometimes happens in response to a particularly stressful competition. Malcolm Gladwell has written an apt description of it, using the 1996 Masters golf tournament as an example. Greg Norman held a big lead,

---

[43] It's interesting to note that a different part of the brain is used for activities upon which you must concentrate (explicit learning) and those which have become automatic (implicit learning). See Fletcher et al. (2005).

then missed a shot:

> With that error, something inside him broke. At the tenth hole, he hooked the ball to the left, hit his third shot well past the cup, and missed a makable put. . . At sixteen, his movements were so mechanical and out of synch that, when he swung, his hips spun out ahead of his body and the ball sailed into another pond. [44]

For an athlete to make it to the top level of a competitive sport requires familiarity with the state of contemplation. To lose access to it is disastrous, which shows the power of the state.

Step Five in Therapy

Every endeavor benefits from the incredible power of the state of Contemplation. The expert therapist can empathize with the client to such a degree that the client unconsciously tells the therapist the solution. It is the effect of the therapist's heart falling upon the mind of the client that allows the client to see what they could not see alone. The therapist's contemplation also actively changes the client by bringing out the client's inner qualities that are touched by the therapist's heart.

Step Five in Music

In musical terms, concentration is shown when the musician plays the instrument with great skill. Contemplation is the instrument playing the musician. We went to a concert of a famous teacher of Kirtan, the Hindu practice of call-and response chanting. The teacher was very skilled and precise, a good musician, but he never let the music sing him. When you know Step Five, you can recognize the moment when

---

[44] Gladwell (2009), pp. 278-279

the musician, with utter confidence in his/her ability, tunes him/her self to the instrument and allows the instrument to guide the musician in playing the music.

> A Sufi's way of contemplation sets the heart in rhythm, which makes even the circulation of the blood regular, and the pulsation and the whole mechanism of the body become rhythmic. When the mind is also set in rhythm by its awakened response to tone, the Sufi's whole being becomes musical. This is why the Sufi can harmonize with each and all. Music makes all things in the world living to him or her and makes him or her alive to all things. —HIK[45]

Step Five in Consulting

One difficulty of this step is that the expertise one has gained is not transferable to another field or type of challenge, yet the person in the fifth step assumes that it *is* transferable. The one who has been successful in business assumes (s)he has found a formula that would work in any business, for anyone.

Most business consultants are experts in this sense: they have discovered something that has worked well for them, in their situation, but they assume they have discovered an absolute truth that will work for anyone. By their advice some people are helped, while others are harmed. For example, a sales trainer who has discovered a powerful sales technique will perhaps not bring success to a business whose ideal is great customer service.

We know a woman who took a course in time management from a consultant who specializes in this. The course

[45] Hazrat Inayat Khan, Vol. 1, The Way of Illumination, Some Aspects of Sufism

assumes that everyone will benefit from time management, and teaches an elaborate scheme of making lists and budgeting time for the greatest efficiency. Our friend is organizationally challenged and assumed this discipline would help her, but she soon abandoned the method. She is intuitive; she navigates her day by a non-logical process that gives her more happiness and accomplishment than she could get by planning her day ahead of time. But the consultant, an expert in time management, doesn't value other solutions. This is a limitation of expertise.

Step Five in IAM

In our school, this step brings expertise with the practices such that they work reliably and intensely, producing energy, emotion, and visions. You can readily apply the insights and confidence you get from meditation to the challenges in your life, producing greater success and expertise.

At this step you feel self-sufficient and successful. Now there is the tendency to underestimate the value of the teacher. You do not feel like a "seeker," you have "found it." As the expert you naturally assume that the teacher is in a similar condition to that which you know yourself. To assume that the teacher is greater than your ideal would challenge your very notion of "ideal." In the spiritual path, many of those who have come this far need a decade or longer to go on.

Step Five in Teaching

At this point you naturally assume that the practices at which you have become adept will work for anyone, and therefor that you can teach others. But at this step you are not yet the teacher; you can only lead others who have the same ideal, because your method is specific to your ideal.

That is, you have found a way that works for you but which may not work for anyone else, and may actually be harmful for some people.

We call one who attempts to teach at this step a "false teacher." This is one who "knows not that (s)he knows not."[46] Such a person is unaware that there is so much more that one should know before teaching those who aspire to know, and in particular, unaware that a teacher needs the ability to match the teaching to the psychology of the student. A teacher at Step Five can be of great help to those who have the same need and background as the teacher has.

At a later stage, Step Seven, you will have both a comprehensive and demonstrable understanding of the teaching *and* a deep insight into the nature of people. This combination produces a true teacher, who can customize the teaching for each student, according to their need, realization and archetype.

It is difficult for a person at Step Five to find a spiritual teacher. Your chosen pursuit is going so well that your ideal is teaching you everything about life, and all that you need to know is that which will allow even greater success toward the ideal.

Examples

Our students have given us many other examples of what the experience of Step Five feels like.

---

[46] There is an ancient Persian children's rhyme: "He who knows not, and knows not that he knows not, is a fool; shun him. He who knows not, and knows that he knows not, is a charm, teach him. He who knows, and knows not that he knows, is asleep; wake him. He who knows, and knows that he knows, is a prince; follow him."

I dove from the 180-foot crane into space, relying on only a bungee rope around my ankles to break my fall; video showed a masterful, fearless, graceful dive. I felt like I was flying; totally and completely free.

❁

I had prepared for this race extensively, both physically and mentally. Ten miles. I knew I could do it, but I was surprised when I got into the 'the zone' right away and stayed in it the whole race, leading to a new personal record.

❁

I was the lead teacher of a high school classroom of 'emotionally disturbed' students; my challenge was to make school enjoyable and stimulating for these students. Most other teachers were afraid of these students, but it was a joy for me. I was proud to see a high proportion of them graduate.

❁

I worked as a volunteer coordinator at a hospital, running a department with a dozen employees and thousands of volunteers. It required diplomacy, tact, political savvy, creation of training programs, conflict resolution skills, and qualities of mind, heart, instinct, and drive. Despite all these requirements, the job came easily. I felt I was able to help each person I worked with to feel at home in themselves, successful, and fully realized, and to work together harmoniously and joyously with my employees and volunteer staff.

Art, Contemplation and the Heart

Artists who create works of deep meaning and impact do so by tapping into the creative power of their hearts. Actors, musicians, visual artists, dancers, poets, and others who make art are in a process of spiritual seeking that spirals in and around the Steps of the heart and mind, through Idealization, into Expertise, and into Unlearning (Steps 4-6), and back again.

The artist must employ Concentration in order to build up technical training in a certain medium, and then to apply those skills to create art. But the necessary next step is to open to contemplation, to lose oneself in one's art. The actor builds his performance through his mind, then releases and allows the role to act him; the musician is played by the instrument following years or decades of intense technical training; the dancer releases into movement that has been carefully choreographed and rehearsed down to every last detail; the poet writes and edits and writes again, jumping back and forth between the spaces of mind and heart. In the end, the aim of a great work of art is to thrust viewers not only into their our own hearts, but into experiences of unity.

A story of expertise from one of our students who is an actor:

> *I was cast in* The Glass Menagerie *as the Gentleman Caller. I decided that I could no longer follow the director blindly, but absolutely needed to do it in my own way—according to my understanding of Stanislavksi*[47]*, my own experiential sense and my own aesthetic. I formulated my discoveries and understandings as a list of principles and methodically worked a process. When the director, whom I respected, worked in ways that I thought were based on a misunderstanding, I adapted them to my own process, secretly. I kept myself on track. I couldn't work with Stanislavski, but I was making a one-man Moscow Art Theatre as best I could!*

---

[47] Constantin Stanislavski (1863-1938) was a Russian actor and theater director, best known for his philosophical approach to acting, which he called 'spiritual Realism'. Stanislavski was a major inspiration to Lee Strasberg, who created the American school of 'Method acting'.

When I couldn't figure out one moment, I went to my teacher, who asked one question: "Where do you breathe?" When we answered that, the whole line of the role was linked up and I just had to stick to my principles, my clear method. I worked to keep myself from being distracted and found ways to deal with all the inner obstacles to staying focused.

Heart Rhythm Meditation is inherently musical, absorbed in the twin rhythms of heartbeat and breath. As they become more regular and rhythmic, the other systems of the body, mind and emotions begin to flow in a more regular fashion, including thoughts and feelings.

A story about expertise in music, from one of our students:

At about age five, I started learning the piano and demonstrated a virtuoso talent. After a long break, I re-discovered music in the last two years of high school. Without too much trouble I got in to a music conservatory, where I studied piano, clarinet, composition and lots of other things. Over the two years that I was at the Conservatory I experienced a very overwhelming emotional response to playing the piano. Playing the piano made me feel more than I could bear. This is not good for a musician; too much feeling stops everything from working properly. Not just that, but I became very angry with myself when the fingers didn't play the music I heard in my head. I would practice and practice and it just got worse. I would experience violent rages directed at myself and the pianos of the Conservatory… and this, along with the full flowering of late puberty and unrequited loves that made me feel constantly like I was about to faint as well as living in an alcoholic household, made it a pretty intense time. Eventually I left in a whirlwind of unresolved emotions and expectations. I never played the piano again.

Though I had a troubled relationship with music as a teen and don't play anymore, I'm a dedicated lover of listening to music. However, my experience of great music is still characterized by 'too much feeling.' When I listen to truly great music—especially live —I almost cannot bear it. It's a feeling like being torn apart by wild horses, a shattering experience, full of feelings of grief and loss. Recently, I was lucky enough to be able to go to lots and lots of concerts at a festival honoring the 250th anniversary of Bach's death. So, I was at a performance of the St. John Passion, a truly truly great performance that put me into a state of disintegration. I was sitting close to the front, and the viola da gamba soloist kept looking over, wondering I suppose if someone was going to call an ambulance. There was an interval, so I sat huddled, shaking in a corner, overhearing people saying things like "Yes, it's good, isn't it!" and "What's the conductor's name again?" The second half contains one of the great moments in Western culture: where Jesus dies on the cross and the words "Es ist vollbracht" (It is accomplished) are uttered first very simply, then in an aria of wondrous beauty and originality. I knew it was coming and braced myself.

Just before the counter-tenor soloist uttered the words, I experienced a presence in the concert hall. I can still feel it as I describe it. First, there was a silence. It wasn't just an absence of sound or a pause in the music, but a Universal silence. It wasn't overwhelming or frightening: not an absence, but a presence, comforting and weightless. High up in the vault of the very high-ceilinged hall I sensed the presence of. . . and I've never said this to anyone before. . . angels. It's difficult and risky for me to say that, because I don't believe in angels, but that's the only way I can describe the experience. There wasn't a feeling of being 'protected' or 'comforted'—just the silence, presence, and this feeling that the whole universe was listening. . .

Puran: For this musician, the next step is to be able to

create a similar experience at will, and I saw right away that it would require him to return to the piano. I suggested to him that he find a piano with which he could begin a relationship. I wrote back to him:

> *Don't sit down and play; that would be like jumping in bed with a stranger. Feel the wood. Strike one key and appreciate the resonance that fills its whole body, right down into its legs. Embrace it and put your ear to its belly. Make a chord and recognize in it the symphony of the heavenly spheres. Make three simple notes with pregnant pauses in between, until tears flow. Then, ask the piano's permission to come back again in humility to seek its favor and bear witness to its divine nature. Do not play any melodies nor awaken that extraordinary pianist within you that has lain patiently waiting; that would be too self-assertive. Let your relationship with the being of the piano deepen in trust until it begs you to give it its voice. Only then, let the piano play you—not to show your skill, but to release the harmonies of its soul that have become embodied in the wood and steel of its body. Let the piano possess you so that it plays itself through you. Do you think it will mind if your technique is imperfect? It longs for the caress of your fingers to coax its beauty out of its shy silence.*

The piano is a metaphor for his heart. But the metaphor works on both levels: his heart and the physical piano can become illuminated together, and the effect will spread throughout his work and his relationships.

Another student, who teaches acting, experienced some insight during the discussion of Step Five that he felt would help him to be a better teacher:

> *I seem to have a knack for inspiring my students, and students often tell me that I am in my element when I am teaching. I have always felt capable and inspired, but also something of a charlatan. Puran's description of how the Expert teaches fits*

with how I feel when I teach. I concentrated deeply on acting for many years, and came to a point where insights would pour out: where I can come up with new exercises easily and make a stream of new connections. But, I realize now, my object of contemplation is not the students; my object is the art form. I can teach many things, and inspire the students with my idealism, but I am not really allowing them to discover for themselves. I am not teaching them in a way that is fully attuned to where they are at and who they are.

We just had a wonderful teacher here who I think is beyond expert. She was able to work with the students in a way that I can't. She wanted to talk to me about the students, not the art form, which showed me that she was contemplating them. She didn't think of what play she wanted to do, but about what would be best for them. She chose monologues individually for each student that were just what they needed at this point in their training. She allowed the students to work in their own way on the show, although she drilled them mercilessly about basic skills. The show was a wonderful success, and the group has taken a real step. Everyone can feel it. They have now achieved very concrete progress and success based on their own individualized work and learning. Under her influence, I have been attending more to the students as individuals, giving them individual time. I've also taken to contemplating them through the heart in meetings and when I write reports. I can feel a difference in myself and in the work. I can feel a different, more mature quality just beginning to emerge, related to the beginnings of a shift from being an expert about the art form to being someone who is more tuned in to the students. I find myself wishing I could feel more what they feel; see things how they see them.

Reflections on Step Five

First meditate and then write about an extraordinary accomplishment: one that you prepared for over a long period of time; that was an expression of your ideal; and that actually happened rather smoothly because it had behind it the incredible power of your heart. By this accomplishment of yours, you showed the greatness of your ideal, and of who you really are.

2 Went to graduate school / met AN
Bryn Mawr
No money
marriage failing
2 children

1 Was in Master Gardener
Program – developed
Spiral Meaning: 8's –
completed the program
while in the midst of
this ideal.

3 Went to IAMU – no money
did it to help my family

Chapter 14
Overview of the First Five Steps

IN THE MAP OF ILLUMINATION, we start out exercising the mind and its power. Then we awaken and develop our deeper faculty, the emotional heart, which has a much greater power. Eventually, we discover a transpersonal spirit that is operating through us. These are three levels of power: the power of the individual, the power of connectedness, and the power of the universe.

Step 1

By "mind", we mean that which processes the senses, reasons, makes decisions and stores memories. From the mind's ability to concentrate comes the power of the mind, called will-power, the ability to decide something that sets one on a path and makes a long-term difference. This is a power that animals don't seem to have; they seem to be generally short-term planners. The ability to place attention on something and hold it there is actually a great spiritual power, necessary for any accomplishment. It is a spiritual power because when you place your attention on something, you direct to it some of the attention of the global mind of humanity. To use short-cut language, your mind focuses the mind of God; you direct the attention of God by your attention. This is the case because there is One Mind, or One Mental Power, that operates through all minds.

The development of concentration and its outcome in will-power is divided into three steps, the first of which is deciding what to concentrate upon. We called this **Commitment**, because it sets our course for a period of time into the future. To this direction, our will-power is applied.

Step 2

The next step in concentration and will-power is developing discrimination, judgment, and relative value. An old friend of mine who had the chair at Carnegie-Mellon University in Psychology told me that the mind is basically wired to make precise comparisons, like between two colors, two pitches, two faces, or the distance between two objects. So the extension of this mental skill of comparison into calculation of relative value between two choices is a basic and powerful accomplishment.

We have used the word **Testing** to mean the process by which we judge and discern value. It gives us the ability to judge whether one thing is better than another. For example, is this relationship better than that one, or is this job or activity or living place, better than some other one. It gives us error-correcting ability, so we can see that we've made a bad decision and reverse course, or confirm a right course.

Step 3

The final step in mental development is knowledge and understanding. If we had to personally test every decision, we would be time-constrained. We need to be able to make decisions on new commitments and choices based not on testing but on understandings from past decisions. We called this **Trust** because we recognize that such decisions are not made from direct experience; they are short-cuts made by generalizing from the past. There is no specific test data on which to base our decision, so we use test data from past events that are assumed to be similar.

One of our students, Melissa, gave us an example with her "white belt experience." She applied something she had learned in Karate class to a new job experience. As she said, "I settled myself and applied my white belt skills—asking for help and trusting that it would all unfold as it should, given concentration and commitment on my part." Her confidence from previous trials in a different domain were applied without considering if they were appropriate for the new domain. This allowed her to reject alternative approaches to her new job, without needing to test these other approaches such as aggression, panic, despair, over-work, or quitting.

The more experience we have with making commitments and testing them, the more comfortable we are with trusting. We are creating our own vision of how life works, which we call "knowledge." Part of our knowledge comes by direct testing experiences, and part by the generalization of those experiences, which is trust that the "laws" we have observed in specific situations are applicable in untried situations. Most of the time, our trust is justified, but sometimes our trust leads to such a disaster that we have to go back and reinterpret our previous experiences in light of the new experience.

For example, if Melissa had failed miserably in her new

job, she might have concluded that her martial arts skill does not apply anywhere else, or that maybe she was not so good at karate anyway, or even worse, that she's not very smart and that other people will not come to her aid. Then that new "knowledge" would be applied in other situations and either reinforced or modified further.

All of this knowledge acquired through testing and generalization is only valid in a "flat" universe, that is, one without extreme features like holes or peaks. It's like Newtonian physics, that holds up very well outside of the forces within an atom or the forces in a black hole, or the inexplicable events of parapsychology.

For example, one can be very knowledgeable about a subject, like economics, until a "black swan" event occurs, like the melt-down of subprime mortgages. (Black swans were thought to be nonexistent, until some were found.)[48] Or you can think you know your husband who behaves in a predictable way for many years through a wide variety of situations, until one day he leaves you without warning, or kills someone, or becomes a monk, or reveals a hidden bank account, and you realize there is an aspect of him that you never expected.

Step 4

There is a hidden side to life that most people see briefly and that few people see usually. It is mysterious, beautiful, awe-inspiring, surprising, and unbelievable until one is transformed by it. It lies outside of one's normal experience; it cannot be seen with the mind. To see the depth of life, one has to be in the depth of one's being. That is what we mean

48 Taleb (2010)

by "heart".

- We call "mind" that faculty in us that observes, compares and remembers the "flat" and obvious dimension of life.
- We call "heart" that faculty in us that feels and operates the profound, hidden dimensions of life.
- Furthermore, we say that mind and heart are the same faculty, just that mind is the surface of this faculty and heart is its depth. Both mind and heart have memory; the memory of the mind is of its observations and the memory of the heart is of its feelings.

The mind creates words and images by which it communicates with consciousness. The mind gives concentration. The heart creates sensations and emotions directly and inspires images to rise into the mind. The heart gives intuition and insight.

The mind gives us the ability to observe the world and, when strengthened through concentration, the ability to accurately discern and compare the differences between one thing and another. The heart experiences the world completely differently. It experiences the effect the world has upon one. It is not objective; it identifies with what it is focused upon. The mind sees other people and things as outside itself; the heart feels within itself the emotions and energies of other people and things. The mind registers the differences between oneself and others; the heart feels the commonness between oneself and others.

The observation of the mind is detached; *detachment* means that what one observes is happening to someone else, not to oneself. The heart does not work by detachment; it produces *attachment*: the experience that whatever is observed is connected to oneself, that the outside world is reflected in the inner world and vice-versa. We call this **Contemplation**. Just as Concentration was developed over the first three steps, Contemplation will be developed over steps four through six.

The opening of the heart occurs in flashes, then in longer sequences that linger and transform ordinary life. It can cause idealistic aspirations, radical and courageous actions, emotions beyond reason or control, blinding passion, surrender of self, and drive to excellence. The opening of the heart makes one unsatisfied, discontent and hungry for the extraordinary.

Step 5

The opening of the heart also unleashes a great power that has the potential to accomplish the extraordinary. When people think of "heart," they usually think of the sensitive side of heart, what we call the left-side: sensitivity, empathy, compassion, gentleness, beauty, etc. But there is a right-side to the heart that gives a person courage, creativity, expression, emotional honesty, and the ability to create and hold a group. The powerful right-side of the heart comes out in Step Five. This power is fundamentally different from concentration and will-power. It works magically, by means that are not linear or even apparent.

The heart acts magnetically to attract and repel people and situations. The heart creates serendipity and coincidence. The power of the heart is desire, that is, love.

Through the attachment of love, the external person or thing is felt within, giving a direct and absolutely accurate experience of the other without coloration by judgment or opinion. This experience gives one a vision of not only who or what the other is now, but also what potentiality is emerging. Therefor Step Five gives one much more information than is possible by observation. The object or other person actually guides one in the process of uncovering its potential.

> *My love for wind power guided me to discover a principle that is more efficient than the conventional designs of wind turbines. My love for computer algorithms guided me to discover extremely rapid ways of analyzing massive amounts of financial data. It was not the cleverness of my mind that found these solutions; the solutions were received from the wind turbine and the computer system by identifying with them and losing myself in them. -Puran*

This is the way all great things are accomplished, through a connection of love. We call this **Expertise**.

These are the first five steps of self-development. They apply to both accomplishments and relationships. These steps may occur in childhood, in adulthood, or after death. A person may be in one step in their spiritual realization, but in an earlier step in their relationships. This is the usual case. A person can be in different steps in relationship and accomplishment.

When a person has advanced to some step on this path, all the previous steps are still active. A person's realization is not assessed by how often they demonstrate the early steps, but how easily they can regain a later step. A person in Step Five, for example, can act like Step Two if they want to, but they can instantly recall Step Five and act from there. In other words, you see a person's realization not from their worst behavior but from the best they can be, reliably.

For example, Susanna was counseling a man who is in a

relationship that is a year old. He was describing his "cold feet." She spoke to him about commitment; they are living together. Then they spoke about testing, and he laughed, "That's us alright, we fight all the time." She spoke about the trust of Step Three and he said, "We're not there yet; maybe we're 2.5." Then she told him about the adoration of Step Four and the ability to see the ideal in his girlfriend. He said, "Oh, I can see that easily. She's a super-woman. I admire and adore her; that's what keeps us together." So he's demonstrating Step Four, not Step Two. Their arguments express his frustration that she isn't living up to his vision of who she is in her heart, and vice-versa for her, rather than a testing of the commitment.

But Step Four, like all even-numbered steps, is fragile; it is a transition step. One must either advance forward to Step Five to make the idealization stable, or fall back to Step Three, which is also stable but mundane, or all the way back to Step One, where he might change his commitment to this relationship and commit to another. If he starts a new relationship, that relationship will have to go through Step One, Step Two and Step Three, but will quickly advance to Step Four, the limit of his heart's development. His relationships can't get any farther than his heart can sustain. One cannot behave consistently above one's realization. One can pretend a politeness, like a fool can act like a great man on stage, but no one can sustain trust, idealization or expertise unless these steps have been realized.

Chapter 15

Step 6: Unlearning

Ring the bells that still can ring
Give up your perfect offering
There is a crack in everything
That's how the light gets in
—from "Anthem" by Leonard Cohen

LIFE IS SUCH THAT NO FALSEHOOD, no pretense can endure, nothing false can go far; it will only go a step and then it will tumble down; it is only the real which will go on. And the more real something is, the less it expresses itself.—HIK[49]

The claim to be kind and sympathetic is like a drop of water saying, "I am water," but which on seeing the ocean realizes its nothingness. In the same way, when a person has looked on perfection, they realize their shortcomings. It is then that the veil is raised from before their eyes and their sight becomes keen. He or she then asks, "What can I do that I may awaken this love and sympathy in my heart?"

[49] Hazrat Inayat Khan, Vol. 10, The Path of Initiation and Discipleship, 1. The Path of Initiation

> The Sufi begins by realizing that (s)he is dead and blind, and understands that all goodness as well as all that is bad comes from within. Riches and power may vanish because they are outside of us, but only that which is within can we call our own. In order to awaken love and sympathy in our hearts, sacrifices must be made. We must forget our own troubles in order to sympathize with the troubles of others.—HIK[50]

Welcome to Step Six, the step of unlearning. You might have sensed this was coming—what progress could there be from the great accomplishment of Step Five, but to tear down the temple and rebuild it?

When you dare to peer from the peak of personal accomplishment into the abyss of personal abandonment, you will find there is no bottom. You cannot descend carefully, step-by-step, into the process of rebirth. You have to jump, with nothing but faith to sustain you.

> Yea, though I walk through the valley of the shadow of death, I will fear no evil: For Thou art with me; Thy rod and Thy staff, they comfort me. —Psalm 23

> *The pine cone of the giant Sequoia tree is smaller than that of a regular pine tree one hundredth its size. These pine cones grow hundreds of feet in the air. The Sequoia lives for thousands of years, and will hold its seeds within those small cones for 20 years until the moment is right. And the right moment is when a fire sweeps through the forest and converts all the smaller trees to ash, leaving unobstructed sunlight for the seedlings of the Sequoia.*

> *Without fire, the small cones do not burst open and scatter their seeds to germinate in this new canopy of light. The forest*

[50] Hazrat Inayat Khan, Vol. 5, Pearls from the Ocean Unseen, The Purpose of Life

fire is the signal to release the seeds of the next generation. It is not a disaster; it is a necessity for the survival of the forest. And the full-grown giant Sequoia trees are not hurt by these fires; they are protected by bark that is as much as a foot thick.

Fire renews life in the chaparral of Southern California as well—stimulating the germination of many plants and clearing away what is dead and old—forming an important part of the life cycle of that ecosystem. Before people settled these lands, they were completely scorched by fire every 25 years or so due to lightning or some other natural event. If these fires are not permitted to burn themselves out, this fire cycle becomes far shorter. Fires occur far more often and unpredictably, without the end result Nature seems to have designed for them.

So it is that the step of unlearning brings one through a kind of fire so that the heart can continue to move towards the next stage in its development. If we attempt to quench the fire before it runs its course, we won't get the result of further expansion into the heart and towards Unity.

Step Six is an even-numbered step; it is not a step in greater glory; it is a step in surrender. The gifts of the previous stages won't go unused—you could not offer yourself in surrender without the experience of victory. When you cannot see at all how to go forward, or even what forward would mean, you can appreciate that you've arrived in a station of great serenity and profound meaning, a place revered by the mystics, who welcome you with celebration.

The sixth initiation is called *the* initiation. —HIK[51]

This is the last step in the formation of the self and the first step in the discovery of the unlimited, eternal and per-

---

[51] Hazrat Inayat Khan, Sangitha 2, Ta'lim, Teaching, Higher Initiations

fect.

The Final Step in Contemplation

After the development of your own point-of-view, in *concentration,* comes the development of another point-of-view. The fourth step is the beginning of the process of *contemplation.* As a person goes into contemplation, several predictable things occur, and those create steps four through six in the path:

4. In Step Four you make the amazing discovery that your vision and understanding of beings depends on your point-of-view. Saint Francis was delighted to notice, as he looked at the trees he passed in the woods, that the trees were looking back at him. When you see from your heart you are amazed at what a beautiful world it is, compared to the mind's view of the same world. Additionally, you can see from another's point-of-view, by which you gain great knowledge and advantage. As two eyes give depth of sight, two points of view, your own and another's, give wisdom.
5. Step Five is the ability to work from another point-of-view or multiple points-of-view, together with the power of confidence and sincerity, and the guide of your ideal. Now you can accomplish great things to demonstrate your ideal in action. Your actions, attitude, and outlook reflect your love for the world, for other people, and for the Higher Power. A person who is pious doesn't talk about his piousness; neither does a person who is creative or powerful talk about these qualities in herself. As you choose to live your ideals rather than talking about them, dishonesty or pretense become impossible.

6. Step Six is the final step in the steps of Contemplation within the heart. At this step, whatever you contemplate has so much reality that your own self is eclipsed by it. You are actually giving your life to your contemplation. Consequently, your own sensations, opinions, and feelings are not important; they cannot guide you any longer.

Step Six in Your Career

The expertise you attained in Step Five is glorious, masterful, brilliant and powerful; the emotion is that of the greatest success. You have been able to express your ideal in a truly extraordinary accomplishment. If you have reached Step Five in a relationship, you've not only met the person in whom you see your ideal, you've been able to make the relationship work and endure.

After some time as an expert, however, you come to a point where you realize that the ideal you have pursued your whole life has not been fulfilling. Your accomplishments don't feel so significant anymore. You say, "Is this all there is?" Your feelings about the insignificance of your own accomplishment extends to others, and so you no longer admire the so-called experts in any field. You come to dismiss reputation, which seemed so important in Step Five.

You have a nagging feeling that there is something you are meant to do, something much greater than you have imagined, yet something you vaguely remember. Steps Five and Six form a pair of milestones: the end and the beginning, the height and the depth of life.

In Step Six, you realize that to discover the purpose of your life you have to get out of the way: you drop your own point of view, letting go of ideas and opinions that limit you. You purify yourself from your own distortions by discounting your opinions, background, education, culture, and everything else that has defined you.

The only way into this greater depth and breadth is to surrender: to accept that you cannot accomplish anything, take a passive position, and allow yourself to be used as an instrument. It is a deep surrender, a letting-go of much of what feels like you. You come to an existential depth where nothing can be said and nothing can be done. Then the object of your contemplation can emerge within you and speak through you. The beauty of the stars speaks through the astronomer. The intelligence and precision of the silicon chip speaks through the computer designer. The innocence and wonder of the child speaks through the educator.

You may mourn the fact that you are losing something you have accomplished, that you have spent immense energy and time building up: a business, a career, a relationship, a body of spiritual knowledge. Consider that no accomplishment really turns out to be worth its cost if you only look outward. The real value of accomplishment is what it has built *in you.* You became great by doing great work, and that greatness in you was the real gain—not the entity that you built outside of yourself. When you consider what you have become through your accomplishments, you will see that the effort was, indeed, worth it.

As you contemplate a much greater accomplishment than anything you've achieved so far, you realize it won't be in your present speciality; you've gone as far as you can in that direction. You are pushed ahead by discontentment and boredom, but you experience fear as you peer down the slope into the valley that separates the peak on which you now stand from the much higher peak that rises above the clouds in the distance.

Think of those you know or of whom you have known who gave up being on top of their game in order to embark on a completely new path—and who achieved incredible successes that no one would have thought possible at the outset. Consider the dark nights these people most likely had to navigate before making the necessary commitment that would lead them to reach the new heights. This dark night is a prerequisite for the dawn of your next achievements and awakenings, as are the strengths developed in the first five steps.

Only by going through Step Six can an expert in one field generalize what he or she has learned and apply it to a greater challenge.

- A labor leader can become a statesman (Lech Walesa).
- A poet can become a President (Vaclav Havel).
- A businessman can become a philosopher (Lee Iacocca).
- An imprisoned activist can rebuild a nation (Nelson Mandela).
- A boxer can become an advocate for peace and social change (Mohammed Ali).

At Step Six, you realize your mind is completely useless in setting direction or goals, yet extremely helpful in navigating once the direction is set by your heart. This is the surrender of your mind to your heart.

The surrender of this Step can feel life-threatening. You experience grief, resistance, attachment, emptiness. One student wrote, "I'm looking for a way out when I should probably be looking for a way in"—a way *into* surrender, *into* the Dark Night of the Soul.

Here is a personal story of unlearning by one of our students:

> *Whenever I am reminded about the Dark Night of the Soul, I look the other way. I feel like I've lived it, survived it and have spent my whole life healing and preventing myself from slipping back into it. The image that came to me this morning was of Kathleen Turner navigating the mudslide in the movie* Romancing the Stone. *I don't want to think that I have to do this in order to move into the next step. Although I am so relieved to have learned how to live and be with pain, this next step really does feel like death to me. There is much fear, lack of reference for the other side. It is hard to imagine, I can't even put words to it. It doesn't feel like an issue of survival, exactly… I can find no reference to make this any clearer right now.*
>
> *As I write, I feel the slippery mud beneath my butt. I'd like and welcome a hand. I want to do this but, my God, I have to make a living and survive, don't I? Can I do both? There is more water now and the mud is running faster but I am still in control. . . I think?*

The Labyrinth of Step Six

This part of the labyrinth shows the difficulty of Step Six. The path descends, representing surrender, from the height of Step Five, down on the left side, representing the mind, to the lowest point, adjacent to the entrance of the labyrinth. This corresponds to the feeling, "I have accomplished nothing in my whole life." The first surrender brings you to a point adjacent to Step One, where you surrender your past fame and future expectations. The rise half-way symbolizes the hope that this discard will be sufficient. But it is not, and the next surrender brings you to the very bottom, where you gladly surrender your understanding and all that you've learned, which you now see as relative knowledge that is obscuring absolute wisdom.

Choosing to Stop at Step Five

Step Six is the valley between the hill of personal achievement and the mountain of absolute knowledge; to descend into this valley will require giving up the confidence and certainty you have gained from a lifetime of accomplishment. Who would choose to do such a thing? You might attempt to ignore your longing for the absolute beyond the personal. You can decide to stay in Step Five; many people do. But if you don't go forward, your heart feels growing frustration, and ultimately, despair and cynicism.

It may seem that the descent and subsequent climb is not worth the effort compared to the comfort of resting on your laurels, but this comes from a place of fear. To justify staying in this place, you may become cynical about efforts to develop further, and may belittle those who aspire to something beyond. However, you know you now sit on the crest of only a small hill in comparison to the mountains, and this causes a kind of grief that your longing will never be satisfied.

Those who are willing to leave their high perch to seek an even greater ideal are rewarded by a purification where their real being emerges from the covers of their personality and culture. The exquisite beauty of real humility brings one to a greater joy of being than any attainment can.

The reality is that resistance is futile. Life itself propels you toward the conscious and dependable experience of Unity, because that is the true reality. First your mind prepares you, then your heart leads you the rest of the way.

The fears of the student are only shadows of death; they are about the shattering of the illusion of individuality. This *dis*illusion is actually duality falling away. With the curtain removed, we can see the light of illumination. In all of this, support is needed; we cannot bear the loss of self without help. We discuss the kind of help that is most needed in more detail later in this chapter.

We reassured our student that, yes, she will be able to continue to make a living and survive, even as she allows herself to become part of all beings. Actually, everything will work better, as you come to know what is true. Trying to operate your life without really knowing that it is one life that is operating *through* you is actually far more difficult.

The Surrender

As you surrender into Step Six, your abilities and knowledge seem to diminish to the point where you cannot accomplish anything. You feel you have learned nothing in your life, and become nothing. You doubt the wisdom of what you knew, since it can't help you out of this condition. Willingly or unwillingly, most of what you had become is stripped away. It seems like a loss, but nothing is ever lost. The object of contemplation has simply become more important than the one who contemplates. A vessel that is full cannot be filled further. Here, you empty that vessel to create space for the next step of becoming.

It is as though you were a sculptor who has worked for a long time on a statue that embodies all of your technical training and artistic vision, a beautiful form that you want to bring to life. You pour your life into this work of art, and it has come to express your ideal. (That is Step Five.) Then you realize there is still something missing in the statue; you have held back something of yourself.

By this point you have come to revere your art so highly as to value the art more than the artist. You feel, as Jelal-ud-Din Rumi said, "The Beloved is all in all, the lover only veils him; the Beloved is all that lives, the lover a dead thing."

> "Greater love hath no man than this, that a man lay down his life for his friends."[52]

This scripture is meant symbolically—to give your life is to give your heart, and to give your heart is to dedicate yourself to another or to a cause.

Upon completing the sculpture, you realize the only way to give your creation life is to give it your own, and you collapse at the feet of your beloved work of art. But the sculpture, now a living, breathing being, lifts you up into her embrace, resurrecting you.[53]

The mystics interpret the teachings of Christ about self-sacrifice this way: that the lover gives up their self-concept—all the defining characteristics of individuality—in order to make a more perfect connection to the beloved. Self-sacrifice is not about giving up something you want; self-sacrifice is sacrificing your thought of being 'other'—your very notion of your self as a separate being.

In psychological terms, the first five steps are about building a self-concept with clear boundaries, and the next four steps are about dismantling it. Why dismantle what

---

[52] The Holy Bible, John, 15:13

[53] This is our interpretation of a wonderful play by Hazrat Inayat Khan. hazrat-inayat-khan.org: Message: Vol. 12, Four Plays: Una: Scene 4

you have so carefully built? Why turn away from your greatest successes and field of expertise? Because it limits you. The willing surrender of Step Six creates the space for this metaphorical death and rebirth. Through it, in love, one is able to become all.

Sacrifice may take the form of a willing surrender, or it may take other forms, like loss, failure, or depression. In all these forms, sacrifice is a kind of crucifixion that always leads to a resurrection. This is the rebirth—the undeniable knowing of your cosmic being that is in touch with all aspects of life and that affects all aspects of life.

Another story of unlearning, this one from Andrea:

This week I am broken and empty. Consumed with contempt for my mediocrity and apathy. I lay awake half the night my mind going around and around from focusing on all that I lack inside and all that I am not able to find compassion for on the outside. And raging guilt through it all—when clearly, I have so much for which to be grateful.

I guess this is a small dark night at the tail end of a long, drawn-out period of ill health and worldly restrictions. I no longer know who I am, and I can't seem to move on from the despair of disliking this obsolete self who is going through motions without any excellence or creative spirit.

It all sounds so dramatic in words. But inside, there is a muted whimper in this yearning. I am not sure I have suffered as much as anyone has suffered; I am just overwhelmed at the disappointment of finding myself so much more ordinary than I had assumed I would become as a child. So much more disconnected from any sense of spiritual community in my daily living than I thought I would manifest by now. This is all really raw and bust open ungraciously. I just don't know where to go or who to be anymore.

> *In recent months, I have been acutely aware of some years of cumulating doubt that I am living as I should be. There is no action here. A paralysis shuts out any light of knowing and I have no story to share of coming through enriched by this today. I'm sick and tired and lost and hurting. And I can't even move on from this voice which tells me that this is pure self-indulgence when externally, this life is so much more blessed with good fortune than most in the world. In the day I can mask it, yet in the dark of the night, I am not living with the Beloved alive in my heart.*

It's actually a sign of an advanced state on the spiritual path to feel such complete and utter discontent. This is cause for celebration. Andrea's heart is realizing that her life is not what it can be.

The rug merchants in the East put out their low-grade rugs for everyone to see. If you are happy with one of them, you can buy it. Only when you demand better, perhaps by saying, "These rugs are not fit for wiping my feet on," do they show you the better rugs. There aren't too many of the good rugs, and they want to reserve them for people who will appreciate them. But the really excellent rug is in the back room, on the top shelf. They won't show it to you unless you insist that what you've seen so far is still rubbish. Then perhaps they'll pull out the heirloom they don't really want to sell. And they'll put a fantastic price on it, to discourage you. But if you can convince the merchant that this rug is the only rug you could possibly accept, and that you respect and admire this rug, recognizing the greatness of the weaver and the one who sells such art, you may get it for a very reasonable price.

Andrea could fall into the common belief that adulthood is about becoming more realistic—about seeing how little a person really can accomplish or change in the world—or she could recognize that the idealism of youth has to be refreshed in adulthood if it is not to be beaten down by the cynicism of the world. The work of the heart is to remember the aspiration of the soul: to fulfill the purpose of your life on earth.

Very few who experience the heart's awakening to the memory of their purpose in life, find themselves in a perfect position to fulfill it. The rest of us fall into dismay that we have gotten off course. The only chance we have to get our lives re-directed toward our purpose is to *remember*. And in remembering what is truly important in life, we have to forget, or unlearn, what is not so important.

The hopeful message here is that there *is* an incredibly exciting, challenging and meaningful work designed just for you. It's waiting for you because no one else can possibly do it. You were born to do it, and you will remember it and dedicate your life to it; as you breathe into your heart, your sense of purpose expands to fill your life.

Discontent with what you've become is a sign of progress. Having this realization is necessary to overcome the "paralysis that shuts out any light of knowing" and come to know the divinity of your being.

Sacrifice and Renunciation

In Step Six we're called to sacrifice our limitations, so that we can love completely and unconditionally. Those limitations are often treasured aspects of our self.

In some spiritual schools, the self is discarded as a limitation, an illusion—even a despised construct of the ego. This is done to attain the relief of liberation. In the path of the heart, the self is dearly admired and valued, and so the self-sacrifice is not a discarding of something undesirable, but *a gift of one's most valued asset*. Do not give up your self because it is worthless, but because it is such a valuable gift to give to the One who gave it to you. What we mean by that is to dedicate your life to the purpose for which you were given life, the purpose for which you were created.

The universe has made an enormous investment to create your personality, your unconscious mind, your emotions, your memories, your skills, and your abilities. It has taken a lifetime to create your ego, or self. This creation has enormous value and will be needed in the fulfillment of your purpose. No part of you should be discarded; transformation is holistic and has no waste product.

We differentiate *sacrifice* from *renunciation*. Renunciation is leaving behind something you no longer want or need, as children do when they outgrow their toys. Sacrifice is giving up something you still value *to gain something else you value more*. If you renounce something, then even if someone were to offer it to you, you would refuse. There is no envy that someone else has it, either; renunciation is not 'sour grapes'.

In a transcendent path, the aim is to renounce your self. You don't want to have a self anymore. In the path of the heart, the aim is to *sacrifice* the self, to the beloved, out of love.

In this vein, our student Elijah Imlay wrote:

> *The real feeling I have is a sense of relief, as if I were letting go of a great burden, any false expectations of myself, waiting for the Beloved to lift me up. Perhaps the real purpose of this practice is to surrender our limited sense of who we are to the great mystery. Knowing nothing, one becomes an empty cup to be filled again.*

Step Six in Spiritual Work

This step has been called "The Dark Night of the Soul" by St. John of the Cross. Though your soul is never dark, it despairs that its instrument, your mind, can no longer be trusted to provide guidance, so you have to feel your way forward like navigating in the dark. It only seems dark because you have closed the eyes of your mind. You are actually coming into a greater light in which you will perceive with your heart a much greater reality, a reality that is universal, not individual.

> What is the sign that one is ready to awaken from sleep? It is when a person begins to think, "All that I have learned and understood seems so unreal; there are some realities of which I am vaguely aware, and yet compared with them, all I have studied and done seems to be of no account." As the dawn comes after the night of darkness, so he sees light appearing; but he has not yet seen the sun; he is only beginning to awaken. —HIK[54]

When you go into the valley of unlearning, you will see what it is you cling to, and that will demonstrate what your faith is. Your teacher will reach out his/her hand to you drowning in the water, offering to pull you to safety. Accept that hand and be saved, for at this step your teacher becomes your savior. Contemplate your teacher and you will gain the understanding and faith of your teacher, which alone you can depend upon. Your teacher has solved the puzzle of passive-volition. (Step Five used volition, Step Six is passive, and the next step is the integration.) "How can I find the ideal of all ideals, when *my* ideal can only lead me

---

[54] Hazrat Inayat Khan, Vol. 12, The Vision of God and Man, Wealth, The Mystery of Telepathy.

to myself?" Instead of being the seeker, allow yourself to be found.

"The one who knows that he knows not, is a charm."[55]

Step Six in Relationships

At Step Six, it is not uncommon to experience the dark night of the soul through a relationship that no longer works. Marriages might break up or a love once returned becomes unrequited. The loss of the beloved may push one into Step Six, or the beloved may choose to depart while one is in the midst of this difficult step. This is not a necessary part of Step Six. The challenge and opportunity of this step is to experience willing, loving surrender, and that's what your relationship is asking of you.

The Lover of All, the Life of our life, wants so desperately for us to experience Herself that She will use whatever or whoever we have grown to love as Her leverage to get our undivided attention. If we have not come to know Her in our beloved, then She will separate us from our beloved so that we might feel Her Love alone. Perhaps then, She might reunite us with Her proxy—the human love we have chosen—or not. Her only wish is to draw us into Union, the Great Awakening.

We see every human relationship as a way of practicing the relationship to the divine. What is it that every beloved finds annoying? The *other*. Knowing this, the mystic wants not to be "other." The seeker of unity wants to experience the beloved as self.

Unrequited love is a common experience of the heart. It can feel like a road leading to a wall with no door, the wall

---

[55] The Persian children's rhyme, mentioned earlier.

of hopelessness and lamentation. You run right into it and reel backwards. Then you get inspired again and take another run at it, smacking into it again. You try to forget the beloved by leaving town, finding another lover, finding a new job... but find that all of these changes feel like further runs at that same wall.

The truth is that those feelings, those physical sensations, and the overwhelming desire felt in an unrequited love are not dreams or phantoms; they are real, and they will lead you to Unity if you do not run away from them, but embrace them fully.

An unrequited love teaches you how to be one with all beings. It plunges you into the agony and ecstasy of universal love—love without boundaries. We humans get to experience love in every cell of our bodies and in every emotion of our hearts. Unrequited love is great practice for this; as there is no expectation from the other, you can come to realize the beauty of loving for love's sake. As Freddie sings in the musical "My Fair Lady," it's enough to just be on the street where the beloved lives—or even in the same universe. In Unity, the beloved is everywhere, and no matter where you go, you're on that street, swooning with love.

Nothing is more real than love—this is not a fantasy! Every emotion can be harnessed to help us feel love more intensely. Every key on the piano can be used to play a love song. As love surges up in you, see it as a gift, whether it is requited or not. Not many people make it this far: to the place where love leads into a greater reality. If the beginner knew what kind of pain love can bring, he or she would never embark on that path.

Our student pointed out how in the midst of fantasy,

dreaming, desire, and pain, people may tell you to snap out of it, to stop with all your dreaming and to step into reality. But the lover *is* in reality—a reality beyond what most people can grasp.

> *I amaze myself at what lengths I will go to deny the idea of actually having met this thing called 'love.' Every rational thought tells me it's not real, it's an attachment, it's a fantasy, it's an illusion, it's just a mental construct.*

Others who don't wish to discover what this kind of love is about may reinforce you in these doubts. Step Six is an invitation to surrender to this love and the pain that comes with it. It is a preview of coming attractions that will be revealed in the Steps of unity (Steps 7-9).

As we travel the path in the context of the relationship to the beloved, we begin by being inspired by an external beloved in the awakening of Step Four. In Step Five, we learn to serve that beloved… and then the beloved disappears in a game of hide-and-seek in Step Six. Now, the challenge is to experience the beloved in ourselves; then, we will be ready to find The Beloved in everyone and everything in Step Seven.

Milestones and Qualities of Step Six

In Step Six, there is a clearing-away of the heavy burden of facts and opinions that have accumulated in your mind, allowing your thinking to shift to a new paradigm. That which has kept your wisdom individualized is being removed. You see that your benefit to others comes not from your opinions, but from the essence of your personal experience.

There is no longer the tendency to argue and push your point of view on others, because you are not sure of the validity of your thinking. This makes it easy to be with others. As you come to have less regard for your own opinions and the opinions of others, you do not see either as barriers to relationship.

Step Five used volition, while Step Six is passive; Step Seven is the integration of the two. Rather than being the seeker, you allow yourself to be found. Rather than having your ideal lead you back to yourself, you become open to finding the ideal of all ideals.

Step Six is a great step forward that is achieved by going backward, a step down into a depth that lifts you up. You are held apart from perfection by the very same knowledge and expertise you have struggled to accrue and held in such esteem. That is, your greatness has become your greatest fault, because it hides the vast potentials in yourself that have not received as much attention. The part of yourself you know so well occludes the part you don't know. Therefor, you have to discount the parts of yourself that work so well, of which you are proud and which have formed your self-identity, in order to uncover the hidden qualities of your heart.

Perhaps, for example, you're a computer programmer and you've made your living by developing that skill, but as a consequence, you've never had the time to experience the musician in yourself, which might be an ever greater ability if it were attended. By unlearning the computer programmer role with which you've identified (but not the programming skill), you can discover other identities.

Listen To Your Body

Spiritual development is all about wholeness, the integration of all parts of your being into one cohesive center.

Much of our being is unconscious, unknown to us, a deep mystery. Our bodies function without much of our awareness. Our minds are mostly driven by subconscious impulses; rational thought is only the surface of an ocean of consciousness. The depth of feeling in our hearts is mostly unplumbed. And the glory of our souls is only dimly recalled.

Outer life is so intoxicating that we can easily fail to see how much there is within us, and we leave our inner life undeveloped. Yet we yearn for the life within, for it gives meaning and purpose to the outer life. So the deeper parts of ourselves send us a message, which often travels through our bodies. When you travel through a Step of power, as in Steps 1, 3, and 5, you experience glorification, and this is relatively easy to deal with. Surrender is much more difficult, and it's here that your body may send you a message to help you enter a step of surrender that you've been resisting. These messages typically take the form of some kind of breakdown, perhaps experienced through an accident or illness.

Some say, "how could the Universe give us illness to teach us a lesson?" It is our own longing to unfold our being that creates the lesson. At first the longing to become sends gentle messages: a dream, an emotion, a sense of potential, a desire, a question. Often these messages are ignored, but the longing of your heart is persistent.

A story of unlearning from Judith Simpson, a teacher, mentor, and retreat guide in IAM:

> *By my 40th spring, I had been through enough that I felt invulnerable, in a way, inoculated against life's tragedies. Having endured some truly difficult experiences, I had come to a*

point where I was teaching meditation classes, developing a community, and guiding students in my own Center of the Sufi Order. I was the director of a nonprofit organization I had founded some years before. It was a heavy load, but no load seemed too heavy for me then. I felt like Superwoman; I felt no sense of having limits. And being very competent, I made sure no one else saw my limits either.

My journey through unknowing began on the flagstones of the front walk to my house, pulling weeds from the flower bed that lined the pathway. Our house had been overrun by carpenter ants that spring, and in desperation (and to my dismay) my husband had called an exterminator who was, at that moment, spraying between the inner and outer walls. I remember looking down at the ants on the sidewalk and having a 'no-boundary' experience: I was inside the consciousness of the ant, I was being invaded by insect killer, the ground felt as if it were trembling beneath me, I lost any sense of my identity. It was the first of many panic attacks, mini-earthquakes that shook the foundations of my carefully constructed personal and professional identity to the core. Mercifully, I didn't know how long this period would persist; didn't foresee that nothing I knew at the time would help me out of it; didn't intuit how much of my life would change before it was finally 'over.' I couldn't imagine that there would be times when my mantra would become my own name; that I would have to remind myself of who I was (or who I thought I was, at least) with every step on the long walks I took to literally ground myself.

The panic attacks and periods of depersonalization increased in frequency. I was barely managing to keep things together. I thought I might have vertigo; once, my physician thought from my description of the symptoms that I had had a stroke. It was clear that I couldn't go on this way, so I began jettisoning some of the responsibilities I carried. I stopped teaching meditation, stopped working with students, reduced my workload... but still, the episodes, and my fear of them, increased.

I thought I was having a breakdown, but oddly, my mind worked as clearly and logically as ever. Eventually, I felt disconnected from everything but my mind, which seemed unaffected. I couldn't find my body in space; I had terrifying periods in which I couldn't connect with any sense of identity; anxiety and fear ruled my waking hours and hideous dreams ruled my sleep. Still, the light of intelligence never dimmed in my mind. With apologies to Descartes: I thought, therefore I was.

I visited a few psychotherapists, none being very helpful. But one psychologist I knew from my own training in psychotherapy, a former teacher of mine, had the grace to both acknowledge that he couldn't help me very much and also to refer me to someone he felt could. Thus I entered into a transformative relationship with a therapist who (after much resistance) convinced me that the route to healing ran through my body, that I couldn't exist as a disembodied soul or untethered intelligence, and that I had to accept my humanity, my history, and my wholeness in order to live and fulfill my purpose on this planet.

For once, I had to accept this hand that was offered to me: interestingly enough, I had to be a lowly ant, knocked off my Superwoman pedestal, and to begin again to construct the narrative of my life. This time, I had to fully acknowledge the legacy of abuse, of hyper-achievement, of chronic fear, and of emotional disconnection that led me to this place. I had to feel the emotions I had run from. And I had to work hard—with everything from karate lessons to dance classes, yoga to hands-on healing—to discover and reclaim my foundation in my body.

It took a long time. Years. My husband fell in love with another woman and left me and my daughter during this period. Our income was cut by sixty percent. My daughter graduated and left for college. I had to take in boarders to help pay her tuition. I was alone for the first time in my life. Thank God, I managed to keep my job—weirdly, I kept getting promoted because I was so skilled at compartmentalizing my life. (It does have its advantages!)

The most difficult aspect of this period was that I couldn't meditate. Meditation, or at least what I knew of it then based on my training, made my state of depersonalization even deeper. I grieved being cut off from the one constant in my life, my source of solace and peace through so many hard times.

I came through it, with humility and trust in my therapist. Still cut off from my mystical roots, knowing I couldn't go back to what I knew of meditation, I reached out to Puran and Susanna. The work of the heart has shown me a way to live as a mystic in this world, this privileged existence. It's given purpose to the 'dark night' I went through, which now seems so necessary to what I've become.

When you say "yes" to the Beloved, you never know what's in store for you. You don't know what you will have to unlearn, or re-learn, or never knew in the first place. You are tested in ways you couldn't imagine. And believe it or not, you're grateful for it.

One cannot know, going into the Dark Night, what it is that is in your way and will have to be repositioned. Those who are devotional experience Step Six as abandonment by God; intellectuals see it as the collapse of rational meaning; the action-oriented feel it as a lack of drive in the face of impossible obstacles. In any case, Step Six will incur the loss of that which has defined you, so that the greater, but unexplored, qualities of yourself can be discovered and developed.

Uneven Progress

Everything you commit to has to go through the same

steps: testing, knowledge, idealization, and so on. When you start a new job, a new relationship, a new hobby, whatever, you have to pass through all these steps with that commitment. It follows that each area of your life—your relationships, your work, your spiritual path—may be at a different step. For instance, you might have had many openings of your heart in regard to relationships, but not in work. One area of your life will lead while other areas of your life will lag.

You might reach Expertise (Step Five) in your career before doing so in your marriage; this is commonly the case. We get a lot more training for our careers than we do for our marriages, and if we love our work, we can eventually reach the ability to create a job that expresses our ideal. We may even achieve wide recognition for this. But it's a very different application of Step Five to be able to create your ideal in your marriage: to be, for another person, what that person needs us to be for their growth.

Progress through the Steps in one realm can promote progress in another realm. Some people hit a wall in their profession and then turn their attention to a relationship, perhaps because the other person is ill or especially needy, or perhaps because they fall in love in a deeper way. Something draws your heart to respond to another person in a way that dissolves your previous barriers, allowing you to feel new depths of closeness to that person. And then that breakthrough spills over to your work, which can now proceed to develop further. The breakthrough of reaching a new step in any area will develop the capacity to live life from that realization in all areas.

The Teacher in Step Six

It is very unusual for anyone to reach Step Six consciously and dependably without a spiritual teacher and practice. Without help, the dark night of Step Six is likely to occur unwillingly, without appreciation for its beauty and necessity. The result is often that the person pulls back from this unfamiliar and scary place, to the comfort of Expertise. We have seen many successful people do this. To make Step Six your base experience, you must honor it and enjoy it, with faith that there is something beyond. This usually requires knowledgeable support from a teacher, or at least from a spiritual path and practice.

If you have found your spiritual path and teacher while in Step Five, the confusion of Step Six will be short. If you're finding your spiritual teacher now, in Step Six, your desperation might enable you to develop this sacred relationship more quickly. If you have a teacher in whom you can put your faith then you can absorb their experience from heart to heart and find your way forward. You are not likely to get through this step without the help of the hand extended in initiation. Even a being like Jesus took initiation from John the Baptist, and no doubt instruction from experienced teachers.

A person experiencing Step Five in a career, hobby, or relationship, is unlikely to seek a spiritual school; everything is going so well. People tend to see the need to find a spiritual school in Step Four or Step Six. If you find a spiritual school while in Steps 1-5, then the progress you make in your spiritual practice will open doors within, allowing for more rapid progress in your relationships and accomplishments.

When you go into the valley of unlearning, you will see what it is to which you cling, and where your faith truly lies. Your teacher will reach out a hand to you as you drown in existential discontent. Accept that hand and you will gain a trustworthy and open-hearted presence in your life who has been where you are and knows the way forward. Contemplate your teacher and you will gain that person's understanding and faith.

Sometimes people confuse the dark night of this step of surrender with a common setback, trauma, betrayal, failure, disappointment, etc. Everyone has difficulties; the dark night is rare. Step Six is characterized by a fundamental challenge to your self-concept that requires you to re-evaluate the Three Big Questions: "Who am I; Who is God, and how do we work together?" If a difficulty does not result in new answers to these questions, then your realization is unchanged, and Step Six is not indicated.

Step Six and Forgiveness

Forgiveness tends to move through a few predictable stages. They don't always happen in exactly this order, but they do progress in this general direction:

1. First, there is the blame of the other for doing something to you, as you would blame a parent who was abusive.
2. Then, there's a progression to a place of excusing the other: "She didn't really know what she was doing; no one taught her to be a mother; she was overwhelmed," or "He was abused himself."
3. After this point, one tries to let go into forgiveness. "I've forgiven him. I don't want to carry this burden

all my life. It was a long time ago, and I'm going to let it go now."

4. Self-criticism might be confused with forgiveness. "I was such a difficult child. It's no wonder my mother used to beat me." Along with this, there may be a more philosophic approach: "No one has a perfect childhood. Household violence is common. No one can hurt you except the ones you love."

5. The final stage of forgiveness—a stage that people usually come to by Step Six—is when you can say, "I'm thankful for all that has happened to me. If one moment had changed, I would not have become the person I am today. All the events of my life have contributed to the process that taught me, awakened me and gave me the experiences of the heights and depths of life. If I had gotten what I thought was best for me at the time, I probably would have created more problems in my ignorance of what I really needed. So thank you, God, for all you've given me. Now that I've seen where Your plan has led, I wouldn't change a thing."

Reflections on Step Six

Have you had an experience of the dark night of the soul, when you could not see at all how to go forward, or even what forward would mean in that situation? Did a new kind of light of knowing appear in the darkness?

Have you ever given up (substantially) everything you loved and had worked to attain? For what?

What have you sacrificed in love? What did you gain?

Have you ever loved someone so much that you set that person free? What happened to your love?

Have you had such grief that you had to surrender your desires, plans, expectations and even your understanding of who you are to the "Way It Is," which means to the wish of "The One Who Is"? What did you get in return?

Have you ever been so desperate that you could not find your way out? Did you accept the hand of someone who saved you?

The following are stories of experiences of a practice called "Diving Into the Heart".

> *I always find it quite hard to touch my tender heart, but this morning, I did it. I was in a minuscule submarine, and the light of my eyes were headlights. Everything was layers of red. I took a good look around my heart and noticed at the back of my heart it was very dark. I shone my light on the walls of my heart and saw deep grooves and little rips. I shone my headlights on the rips and gouges and the light was like a laser, healing me. The back wall of my heart lightened. I looked into the bottom of the back of my heart… it felt so sore and tender and I bathed it with my tears.* —Paula Roome

> *I have tried this practice a couple of times now. On the first occasion, as soon as I looked in, this voice inside said, "Oh no!" As my eyes penetrated deeper, I inwardly heard the words, "Coming in, no hiding now!" And then these words came: "Free the inner voice, speak of this love." I saw a black mark on the inside of the bowl. With a little bit of attention, it rubbed away. It was a golden cup that held treasures beyond price. I felt a strong sensation, an opening at the back of my heart… This morning, diving in again, I saw this person drowning, waving, calling out, "Save me, save me!" My instinct was to reach out and offer a hand… but then, I realized who it was and I let her drown. Goodbye. There is no room for two in this cup. The cup is no longer inside me; the cup surrounds me. I am in the cup, drowning into the waters of a bottomless ocean. Inner and outer merge. The cup disappears.*

In another meditation, as I lower my head to look within, an opening appears, like a parting of water. I see the same figure, 'me,' thrashing around in the ocean, flailing arms, crying to be saved, but drowning. I watch her sinking, I see her going blue in the face, struggling, dying, unable to breathe anymore. She vanishes, out of sight. Then I lift my head and dive into my heart once more. A blaze of orange fire followed by a vision of a yellow sun rising. —Anon.

No deaths needed!
Death of David shatters
all constructs 2004.
10 significant deaths followed
in the next 8 years.
Grief work took me
into my Art where
the unconscious was
made conscious.
The Dark Night of the
Soul was captured in
"Find Me in the Hills"
series from 2004 – 2009
Resolution Series followed.

Chapter 16
Step 7: Unity

The mystics contemplate the Being of God, and so raise their consciousness above the limitations of time and space and liberate their souls by lifting them to the divine spheres. – HIK[56]

STEP SEVEN IS THE BREAKTHROUGH of unity consciousness. It is experienced as the ultimate freedom, the freedom from being bound in one time, one place, and one identity. Until now, you have experienced the divine *qualities*, such as insight, wisdom, compassion, loyalty, peace, joy, sacredness. Now you experience the divine *Being*, the One to whom those qualities belong. As your being is greater than all your skills, talents, expressions and contributions, the Being of God is infinitely greater than the divine qualities.

That which you have pursued all your life, the ideal of your heart, is now seen as a limitation, a personal ideal, beyond which stands the unity of all ideals. To proceed further in the path, you have to aspire not to what you think is best for yourself, and not even for what you think is best for humanity, but for what the heart of humanity wants for itself.

---

[56] Hazrat Inayat Khan, Sayings, Nirtan, Aphorisms

> The further initiation, which is the seventh, is a stage where a person even rises above the ideal (s)he has made. (S)he rises to that perfect Ideal which is beyond the human personality, which is the perfect Being. — HIK[57]

> A mystic can only be called a mystic when he or she has arrived at the stage where their ideal is larger than that which can be covered by a name. They may give any name to their ideal, but if they cover their ideal with a name they have certainly not yet arrived at the mystic stage. — HIK[58]

> The Sufi knows that progress in every direction in life depends upon the ideal. As high as is the ideal of a person, so high (s)he rises in life. Then in the end (s)he sees that each ideal was made by him/her self; (s)he is the creator of every ideal that (s)he desired to attain. But the ideal itself is a limitation of the perfect Being, because there is you and me in it. Then the breaking of the ideal comes as the final attainment when the ego realizes, "I am All." — HIK[59]

> Shatter your ideals upon the rock of truth. — HIK[60]

Your ideal is like your vision of the mountaintop of human possibility from a place in the valley; you see a face of the mountain clearly, but not the whole mountain, so you

---

[57] Hazrat Inayat Khan, Vol. 10, The Path of Initiation and Discipleship, 1. The Path of Initiation

[58] Hazrat InayatKhan, Vol. 11, Mysticism in Life, 6. The Ideal of the Mystic

[59] Hazrat Inayat Khan, Vol. 5, Pearls from the Ocean Unseen, Sufism

[60] Hazrat Inayat Khan, Sayings, Vadan, Boulas

see only from your own point-of-view what possibilities lie in the heart of human beings.

Step Seven is the experience of reality itself; not reality as it looks from any single point-of-view, but reality independent of the lens through which reality is seen. It is the experience of all ideals, beyond the individual conception of ideal. It is startling, surprising and bewildering, because the experience of the whole can not be anticipated from the experience of only a part, no matter how great that part is.

In the full and complete experience of reality, there is no division into "mine," and "yours," nor "good" and "bad." Those divisions are lines drawn in the sand by the discriminating faculty of the mind.

> There is nothing either good or bad, but thinking makes it so. — Shakespeare[61]

Only through the heart can the experience of unity be approached, because the heart accommodates all, is a part of all, and this emotional acceptance is a prerequisite for the experience of all.

Emotional Wholeness

Emotional wholeness is a characteristic of the experience of unity. It is feeling the emotion of all emotions. If human emotions are seen as the keys on a piano, most people stay in the middle octave, the middle range of emotion. People can handle happiness, but not too much—certainly not ecstasy, which is suspect as mania. And some little sadness can be felt, but not too much, lest one fall into depression. As long as one fears one's own emotions, one cannot possibly expand one's emotional range into the powerful, cosmic

---

[61] William Shakespeare, Hamlet, 2.2.259

emotions expressed, for example, in Handel's *Messiah*.

The main impediment to the experience of the Whole Being is one's fear of the whole emotion. One aspires to experience peace, love, and joy, but these are each parts of the whole emotion, and no part gives the experience of the whole. To have the experience of God, you must be willing to have the emotion of God, and that emotion is all emotion. It includes perfect peace, unconditional love, and unending joy, and also includes endless longing, incomprehensible betrayal and inconsolable grief. If any of the emotions are suppressed, then part of God is rejected and the experience of unity is denied.

Emotional wholeness can be safely handled and should not be feared because the heart which experiences the whole emotion is not your personal heart, it is the Heart of All. The Heart of All can experience the emotion of all; that is its constant reality. To attain Step Seven, you have made a leap of faith that the emotion which you are willing to feel will be such a perfect mixture of joy and sorrow, peace and pain, that the entirety of it will be intense, but safe.

You can see why the development of the heart is a prerequisite to the repeatable experience of unity. You can have a peak experience of unity without opening your heart, but it will likely be so overwhelming that you will fear it recurring. When the capacity of your heart is expanded, the energy and emotion of the whole experience of Being will be welcomed and revered.

The True Teacher

With the experience of unity in Step Seven you can teach anyone, of whatever archetype, belief, or ideal, because you can appreciate all of the variety of human aspiration. You can help a person along their own path, even if it is a different way than your own.

> The wise one agrees with both the foolish and the wise; (s)he is ready to understand everybody's point of view. It may not be his or her ideal, or way of looking, but (s)he is capable of looking at things from the point of view of others. It is not one eye that sees fully; to make the vision complete two eyes are needed, and so the wise one can see from two points of view. If we do not keep away our own thoughts and preconceived ideas, if we cannot be passive and desirous of seeing from the point of view of another, we make a great mistake. This third stage gives a tendency to understand every person we meet. —HIK[62]

Stage Three is the experience of unity through Steps 7, 8, and 9. Though these steps are very close in concept and beyond the reliable experience of most people, everyone has experienced these steps as peak experiences. Step Seven is an awakening that begins a new stage of life in spirit, just as Step Four was an earlier transition that began the stage of life in the heart.

The opening of the heart in Step Four changed the relationship you have with the world, revealing your ideal, a reflection of your soul, and therefor a defining characteristic of your individuality. Step Seven is a step of awakening that reveals the Absolute, an experience that is unfiltered by individuality; it is *non-dual*. "You" are not present — though you are aware of an amazing and magnificent experience, it does not seem to be your *own* experience. You are *sharing in the experience the universe has of itself.*

---

[62] Hazrat Inayat Khan, Vol. 14, The Smiling Forehead, The Soul, Its Origin and Unfoldment, Spiritual Attainment

One experience of unity will not change your world-view; the experiences that have shaped your self-concept and view of reality are too deeply entrenched. Only through repeated exposure to the reality of the One Being do you begin to see that your entire notion of who you are and what is the nature of life must be reorganized to accommodate the much wider view of reality that is emerging in you.

In the Stage of the Mind, Steps 1, 2, and 3, the world is observed from your own point of view. When you concentrate your attention on something, there is a duality between subject and object, observer and observed. In the Steps of the Heart, Steps 4, 5, and 6, the world is experienced through another point of view in contemplation, where you *become* the object you concentrated upon. It may seem as if you have overcome duality because the experience is so completely different from your own point of view, and because the power of contemplation is astonishing, but you are still an individual being that is observing and interacting with the world; although from a different point-of-view. That's still duality; in unity there is no individual.

In the language of the mystics, we would say that you are having a direct, personal, experience of God, not God as other, but that which is within you and that you are within, eternally. You do not feel at this point that you are experiencing yourself, rather you are aware that your experience of God is allowing God to experience Herself.

The Progression From Step Five to Step Seven

The transition from Step Five to Step Seven is one of the most difficult because the power of the ideal is very great, and the power of reality is even greater. In between these mountains there is a deep valley where everything must be questioned.

Susanna's story of this transition:

I studied psychology at the University of Vienna, where Sigmund Freud had lectured, because I was fascinated by the descriptions of my high-school teacher of mental illnesses she had worked with. I wanted to know how people became mentally ill. Furthermore, I wanted to know what the soul is, as "psychology" literally means "the science of the soul." There was an idea that mentally ill people were experiencing their souls more intensely, as a lot of mystics and saints had been mentally ill.

Over my five years in the university I had several internships in mental clinics. But after my oral exams, which I passed, I was struck by the limited career options open to a Ph.D. in psychology in Austria at that time. I would be employed to conduct patients through batteries of tests to determine how they were mentally and emotionally impaired. At that time there were no treatments except for drugs, and there was no attempt to discover how the illness developed or how it might be cured.

I was so disappointed by the lack of understanding of the emotions in psychology and the lack of interest in the nature of the soul that I decided to leave the field. I fell into theater by accident, and spent several years as an actress and director. I learned more about myself, and energy, and states of being in theater than I ever did in psychology. But I was never committed to theater; I was always terribly scared by it. It never felt like it was my purpose. After several years I was led to meditation, and finally to my teacher, who taught me a method by which I could actually experience my soul and the souls of others.

The experience of the soul occurs in Step Seven. Puran has a story to tell from his own life.

In 1968, I visited some good friends in prison who were serving five-year sentences for having resisted the draft. We had worked together in the peace movement. At that time, the inmates in this minimum-security prison didn't wear uniforms, just their street clothes. And there was not a separate visiting area; visitors could freely mingle with the inmates in the prison yard.

As I was visiting with my friends, another prisoner came up to me, excited to see me. He shook my hand enthusiastically, welcoming me — he assumed I was a new inmate. When he realized I didn't recognize him, he said, "Well, I sure recognize you. You're the one who convinced me to turn in my draft card! So what happened to you? How long are you in for?" I had to say that I had not been indicted. I had fully expected to be sent to prison; my wife and I had even had a daughter based on my idea that it would help us keep our marriage together while I served time. But some mistake between my draft board and the federal prosecutor had enabled me to slip through the cracks.

I had urged others to do what I did, and although it hadn't hurt me, it had caused extreme suffering to those who followed my advice. I never visited my friends in prison again. One of my friends came to visit me after he was released from prison; he was a broken man, damaged by isolation and sexual assault. "What have I done?" I thought. "In the name of peace, I have caused suffering." I had taken action on behalf of my pacifist ideal, but it had caused harm to others. There seemed no other choice but to abandon this ideal that had so shaped my concept of self and my life choices. I dropped out of the peace movement and entered the dark night of Step Six.

I was desperately searching for the truth — a year later I was found. I can't say I found my teacher; in truth, he found me, as it is always.

> Ye have not chosen me, but I have chosen you, and ordained you, that you should go and bring forth fruit.[63]

We think of ourselves as seekers, but our seeking is bound to fail; we must allow ourselves to be found. That is Step Seven.

Another story of how taking action on behalf of your ideal can lead to surrender, came from a friend.

> *I had been working for several years for a powerful official in the Executive Department of the U.S. government when I was asked to help clean up an environmental problem: thousands of gas stations and oil storage facilities across the country had old, underground tanks that were leaking petrochemicals, contaminating soil and groundwater. I did the background work that went into a new federal law that required all leaky tanks to be replaced, then I tracked down the violators. As a direct result of my actions, 40,000 small companies were put out of business because they couldn't afford to replace their tanks. I later discovered that many of the companies I forced into bankruptcy were bought up at bargain rates by a corporation controlled by my boss, who was then able to get legislation passed that allocated federal funds for replacing the leaky tanks.*
>
> *I was outraged; I thought I was serving my ideal, but I had been used in a scheme to enrich a corrupt government official. I quit my job and testified in Congress against my former boss. Nothing was done about it and I was personally threatened. I descended into a dark night of unknowing.*

Another example is from a man we knew in the 1950's:

> *When Steve was in graduate school he became involved in a cause of social justice and strongly advocated an action that*

---

[63] The Holy Bible, John 15:16

would help people at the lowest levels of income. Then he discovered that the leaders of this effort were secretly members of the Communist Party with an agenda that he found repulsive. Steve felt betrayed by his ideals and thereafter turned his full attention to science. He became a significant contributor to his field and remained suspicious of idealism in political and economic affairs.

The Step Six view is, "I don't know how to help the world, or anyone. What I try to do goes wrong. I don't even know what's good for me or how to attain peace in myself." The challenge is to see that the evolution of humanity *is* taking place, in ways we don't understand and by means we don't recognize.

The sacrifice of Step Six is a sacrifice of one's self-concept. There is nothing to do and nothing to say. However, there is hope, revealed in a kind of optimism: "I trust there is an inherent spark of spirit and light of good-will that will somehow emerge in people in critical moments. If we are deserving of peace, then peace will come to us eventually." To create a world of peace will require the understanding of the whole world, not the partial understanding of a person in the world. Reality is complex and people are hard to help. Can you really see what is going on and in what way help is needed?

To illustrate the problem of trying to be helpful with limited understanding, consider this classic Sufi teaching story.

You are traveling with your spiritual teacher, who has agreed to let you accompany him in his work if, and only if, you do not interfere with or question his actions or behaviors.

Together you come to a river that is too wide to swim, and you hail a passing boat to get a ride. While sailing across, your teacher disappears and you find him in the hold, drilling holes in the bottom of the boat! As you near the opposite side of the river, the boat sinks in shallow water and the two of you manage to wade safely ashore.

Soon, you come to an old city that is surrounded by a crumbling wall. Tired and ready for a night's rest, you ask for accommodations, but the people are hostile and refuse you. As you leave, now exhausted, your teacher insists on stopping to rebuild a section of the city's wall, and he persuades you to help.

After walking many more miles together, you and your teacher find yourselves welcomed to a kingdom whose king seems to already know your teacher quite well. You are both treated as honored guests, and you're even taken on a horseback ride with the king and his son, the prince. At one point, you, your teacher, and the prince are separated from the group, and you watch in astonishment as your revered teacher purposely causes the boy's horse to buck him off. The boy's leg is broken, and you are forced to make a quick getaway with your teacher on horses that don't belong to you.

Completely bewildered, you burst out at last, "I'm obviously not capable of understanding your work… would you please explain why you sunk the boat of the kind captain that gave us a ride, repaired the wall of the people who threw us out, and hurt the son of our generous host?"

"These things are not as they seem," your teacher replies. "A band of pirates was coming down the river, and they would have commandeered the boat if it had not sunk; as it was, the captain was able to repair and keep his boat. As for the wall, there was a treasure hidden in the city wall by their ancestors, and by repairing the wall we preserved the treasure for a future generation that perhaps will be wiser and less belligerent. And the prince whose leg was broken has a cruel heart that would have made him a wrathful ruler. The law in that kingdom is that the crown is passed down from father to son, pro-

vided that the son is of sound body. The boy will walk with a limp, so the lineage will pass to his younger brother, who is far more kind."

The world is not random; it is governed by those who can see beyond their own desires and opinions to appreciate the wisdom of the One who creates, sustains, destroys and re-creates the world. Vast consciousness and evolved realization are required to understand what is right and what is wrong, how we can help and when to stay out of the way. In Step Seven, your action does not come out of an enthusiasm to promote your own ideal, nor does non-action come from lack of concern or hope. All action comes from a developed consciousness that enables us to see what *is,* rather than seeing the world through the lens of the self.

The teacher in the story above chose at times to override such ideals as honesty, respect for the property of others, non-violence, and so on, because of his larger vision. This can only happen because your beloved ideal, which you discovered in Step Four, and for which you dedicated your time and energy in Step Five, was shattered in Step Six. From the broken shards of your ideal emerges an absolute ideal, greater and higher then anything you have known before.

People who have not been through the unlearning of Step Six are promoting their own agenda, based on their personal skills, desires and understanding of the need. Although this may not help the Cause directly, all that people do is valuable, if only because it is practice in discovering their ideal and learning to apply their heart to accomplish what they wish to accomplish. In Step Six one is passive, then in Step Seven one is active again, impersonally.

Puran has a story to tell of a powerful experience of Step

Seven that occurred on a retreat.

> *I was on retreat in the Swiss Alps with my teacher, Pir Vilayat Inayat Khan. This was a group retreat, with hundreds of people attending from all over the world. I went on retreat alone, farther up the mountain in a remote cave. Though it was isolated, I could feel the vibration that had been created by many other spiritual seekers who had used this cave for the same purpose over the years.*
>
> *After a week of meditation, I entered an incredible inner space of peace and power. I walked back down to the camp. Pir Vilayat was leading a meditation outside when I returned. He looked up and saw me walking, and was so struck that he stopped speaking in mid-sentence. Afterwards, he told me, "I couldn't believe it when I saw you. You appeared to be not walking, but floating. You were part of the landscape, not a person at all." This was the outward appearance of my Step Seven experience.*

Integration of Source and Self

Realizing Unity requires integrating your concept of God (the All, the Source, the One Being, the Absolute, the Higher Power) with your self-concept. In Unity, there cannot be a dualism where matter is separate from spirit or the self is separate from God. A separate relationship is expressed in such slogans as "God proposes and man disposes," or the Christian song with the words, "He is great and I am small." To separate God from self is to create an unhealthy, internal division that does not exist in reality. It prevents one from the full realization of one's limited and unlimited aspects.

An ancient attempt to overcome dualistic thinking is to assert that in reality there is only pure consciousness, and all else is its imagination. In particular, in this view, the self is an illusion. Indeed, in meditation, one can experience a universal consciousness beyond self and non-self, space and non-space, time and non-time. There is no worship in this view since there is no worshipper, and no Creator, but there is reverence for those great beings like the Buddha who have demonstrated the dissolution of self.

But the attempt to assert unity by denying the material half of the duality is unsatisfactory. It is like a physicist proposing a unified theory of atomic forces and gravitational forces by saying that gravitational forces are illusions. There would be a simple solution to a unified consciousness if individuality did not exist, but denying the self misses the purpose for creation.

Something is gained by drawing the universe into a focus — when a pool of still water is stirred into a whirlpool or a drop of water is frozen into a crystal, hidden aspects of the nature of water are revealed. We could say there is nothing but water in the whirlpool and the snowflake, but then we would blind ourselves to the incredible power and beauty that these manifestations of water reveal. Similarly, if we deny the existence of individual consciousness we will know less about the nature of consciousness and how it operates.

Furthermore, non-dual approaches end up disparaging some aspects of a person, like the ego, which is needed to take responsibility as a co-creator. Mystics have wrestled with the question: "Does the Creator have a need for the creation? Can an individual contribute anything to the universe?" If not, then what is the purpose of creation? If so, then doesn't the individual bear some responsibility? If there is individual responsibility, then there must be ego. A holistic understanding can exclude nothing.

A third approach, the path of the heart, leads to an integration that honors both self and God, yet does not make God 'other' than self. The heart's view integrates both spirit and matter as aspects of One Being. It reveres a Creator, but not as a separate entity from creation. We do not even see a separation such that God is the invisible and self is the visible, or that God is the infinite and self is the finite. There is no point in reality where a line can be drawn that demarcates self from God.

The Way to Unity is Conscious Breath

Conscious breath unites the levels of reality, from the most invisible and abstract to the most material and specific. The Creator is continually being expressed and circulated through creation, which is dynamically updated in each creature. The stream of life flowing through us that connects the infinite and finite in our being happens with each breath, refreshing each one with Oneness.

God is a *continuum* that includes the whole spectrum of existence, and the self is also a continuum. The paradoxical experience is that the Being whose Presence you feel all around you, is also emerging within you as yourself.

The hallmark of Step Seven is that the state of meditation becomes reliable. Upon closing your eyes and breathing consciously, you are conscious of an undivided reality that is conscious of you. You are experiencing the ocean of consciousness that gives rise to the waves of individuality. The wave that is you exists in this oceanic experience, *and* that wave is nothing but ocean. Throughout, you are aware of your heartbeat, broadcasting the rhythm of the cosmos. No aspect of reality is denied in this universal meditation. Neither does your self disappear, nor does the universe disappear. Spirit is present, and matter is present, yet spirit and matter are not separate; matter is the frozen state of spirit, like ice and water.

The person in Step Seven is "one who knows not that he knows." Now you have real knowledge and undeniable experience. You are now in a position to satisfy the longing of your soul.

Experiences of Unity

The experience of unity is unique for each person and different each time it is felt. Yet it has unmistakable universal hallmarks, as we discussed above. Here are a few examples of the peak experience of unity that eventually leads to the base of a Step Seven realization. See if you can feel the similarities between these stories. Do they touch upon your own experience?

> *I went to a place that I interpreted as either being pre-birth or maybe even preconception. The sun was very bright, warming and nurturing. I had the feeling that everything was beautiful and perfect.*

❁

> *I felt a galloping terror, an approaching death, then I 'died'—and in that instant glimpsed an utterly black essence of Reality, condensed into a point, which then exploded at unimaginable speed in ten directions and ten dimensions, expanding infinitely rapidly and developing complexity at an infinitely fast rate. As my self regathered, I tried to take in the journey: staggering bewilderment! I couldn't speak. I raved. The only reference point I had was Arjuna asking Krishna, in the Bhagavad Gita, to show him his Cosmic Form. Krishna refuses three times, but eventually reveals it. Arjuna, unable to bear it, raves, raining superlatives upon superlatives and not coming close. I had visions of mandalas and images of The Throne and of Ancient Egyptian architecture.*

Vast, illuminating, all-pervading, wipe-out. . . On the second day of a retreat I ventured down into the town to go for a run. Shortly into my run I fell into the awareness that I was everything. I remember most being the green grass, being the house, I remember being the inside of the house, the colors and textures of the rugs and furniture. I also remember feeling blissful and peaceful. The experience gradually faded as I continued my run; however, there seemed to be some sort of aura left over. When I returned to the retreat center, I felt unable and unwilling to talk. As I was coming up the stairs, I met one of the retreat guides. The words that came out of my mouth were, "This is about love, isn't it?" She looked deep beyond my eyes and nodded her head. Her face was light.

This morning I was sitting outside in my yard meditating. As I breathe in, my breath comes to my heart through all that exists, and as I breathe out, my breath fills all things, creating and giving life. I feel like the universe has no center, just one huge body, then I feel like there is a center to this oneness: my own heart. I want to rely on this feeling in everything I do.

A meditation on an ocean of love: I threw myself in, drowning. I became the ocean, then began to feel myself crashing on the shore, resting on the land below, feeling all things at once.

I felt my heart pounding as the center of the universe and the flow of light in all directions. Then a clear, quiet peace descended.

The experience was 'of' infinity and 'in' infinity. I didn't 'feel' anything, though afterwards there was a sort of shock that I had experienced something on a mythic scale. The thing I remember most was infinite vastness, 'place-less-ness' and of being utterly alone in the universe. But this wasn't a feeling of 'me' being alone in the universe. I didn't suddenly feel alone or lonely, but all the identifiers of identity were missing.

A Unity Experience by Elijah Imlay:

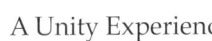

I had my first mystical experience—defined as a direct experience of the universe without an observer—at age 19. It was an experience of stages of illumination in which the world around me dissolved first into energy and then into light, and I saw that everything in the universe, including the 'I' that I had identified with, was made of light. 'Dissolve' is not quite the right word; I was able to see what physicists say is actually there. The lightning through my crown removed, in one flash, all mental and physical constructs. They all ceased; what remained is impossible to describe. It was like being the essence of Light itself, both the source of all light and also the manifestation of that light—such that there was also (somehow) the awareness of the individual existence that subsists within and is inseparable from the Great Light. The Great Light could also have been called the Great Sound, because they were One, but what came back with me into incarnation was Light.

At a retreat, I had a second Unity experience. We were taught to be passive to the actions of the Divine Being upon us. When I repeated a sacred word, it was as if the Beloved were repeating the word. What I had assumed was my breath was really the Breath of the One Being. I experienced God not as a remote or abstract ideal, but as undeniably present everywhere at all times, a message of love—and the purpose of creation is to manifest that love. This retreat was a continual act of glorification in which every atom and every cell of my body, every thought, and every feeling participated together as One. Felt on the breath, these exalted feelings did not disappear into oblivion; without any loss of attunement, their glory descended on the breath into an effulgent radiance, kind of like turning a human being into a star. Only this star was not distant, it was here, and it was the Light of Love. The effects of this Unity experience lasted for a while, perhaps a few months. What persisted was the gift of being able to 'tune in' at any time: not only while sitting down to meditate, but while brushing my teeth or carrying on a conversation.

If you are meditating with a flower in a Step Seven realization, you will have two kinds of experiences, which we call Contemplation and Meditation. In Contemplation, you can feel yourself *being* the flower, feeling what the flower feels when it basks in the sun and rain, pulls nutrients from the soil, and produces beautiful colors and textures.

Meditation takes you even farther: you would experience not just this rose, but rose-ness, the essence of rose, the soul of the flower — the divine qualities of beauty, grace, perseverance, and much more. This is the experience of spirit becoming manifested as a flower. Beyond rose-ness is flower-ness, the essence of all flowers, which then opens up to the essence of life, and then to the life of life, pure spirit. The flower and your self are both present, but your being is neither flower nor human; you are both, and the spirit of both, and all that is spirit. The flower is a portal through which you enter into infinity.

When we contemplate another person, we can feel what it's like to have the body that person has, to think the way that mind thinks, to see through those eyes. It's remarkably accurate, not at all like the mixture of projection and fantasy that occurs when we think about others from our own perspective. But when we meditate together in the unity state, we can feel what the other person experiences in meditation:

the qualities of their heart and soul, the forces of subtle energies and how they circulate in that person, the way the universe is discovering itself in a new way in him or her.

In the state of unity, you are the flower, you are the being of another, but you are more, you are that which becomes those beings, which permeates them and incorporates them and yourself, into a wholeness. This is not just a *different* view, as through another's eyes; this is a *universal experience.*

Appreciation For the Journey

We hope you have come to realize how valuable is every experience in life. Life is pulling us through the path, whether we appreciate it or not. What seems like a terribly hard time of confusion, destruction and loss can be the catalyst for the change that we most need. The downs prepare us for the ups. We couldn't see this if we didn't have the Map. Stuck in the circles of the labyrinth, we wouldn't realize the progress being made, especially when we come to Step Six—where we seem to be only a tiny distance from the point where we entered the labyrinth, yet we're actually on an advanced trajectory for the future and a permanent graduate of the lessons of the past.

We can let life pull us through the labyrinth, perhaps with delicacy and subtlety at some times, and with harshness and bluntness at others—or we can take the process in our own hands and operate it skillfully in the context of a spiritual retreat. On retreat, you can experience with conscious intention what life would otherwise have to arrange, relieving yourself of the slow and often painful process of the unconscious way of walking, and ensuring that you make the transition from one step to the next without backtracking. Rather than moving in loops that can feel like a kind of purgatory, you get the needed prod of advice and loving support from a teacher to step onto the next foot.

This is not to say that loops are not appropriate sometimes. As you begin to grasp the way in which one's path can dance around the labyrinth, you may begin to see how Step 4 (Idealization) and Step Five (Expertise) can progress with great energy into Step Six (Unlearning) and dissolve, leading to another run of Step Four and Five that may repeat many times.

Our student Andrea, whose writings throughout offered a rare combination of eloquence, empathy, kindness towards the self, and passion, wrote:

> *I'm stuck in the existential quicksand of Step Six… my confidence to do or say or go anywhere is shattered. I don't have any idea what my idealized action would be, what would be worthwhile to say or where I should go.*

Again, let us reiterate that while the Step Six state is difficult and disruptive to workaday life and relationships, it is also a very advanced state that merits great respect. On the other hand, it is something to be moved through, not to become mired in. Use your intuition to guide you into Step Seven; remember the experiences you've had of unity, however fleeting, and work to experience more of that state in meditation. As you build your access to the state of unity, don't forget you have work to do.

Consider what it is the world needs and what you're passionate about doing. There is something you're being called to do. You may need to retreat from Step Six for now and get back into action. Ask your heart what it is you're not looking at that urgently needs to be done. There is no loss or setback in your spiritual progress by doing this, for these

Teach again

steps have no fixed time requirement. You might breeze through Step Six later.

You may feel a certain fear of returning to a way of working and being that is obsolete for you now, of numbing down in the juggling of tasks, returning to being a kind of duty-bound automaton that comes only from a place of individual willfulness. Your challenge is to work in a new way, driven by your heart—where you'll avoid the 'should' and save your precious heart for the 'must.'

Sometimes spiritual advancement comes through retreat, sometimes through advance. Do you have regrets and things you'd like to attain? Then use your spiritual power to attain what your heart wishes. Follow your heart without hesitation. Just be sure that what you do, you do because you love it, and you do it in a way that demonstrates the extraordinary being you are. Do something that no one else can do, combining everything you know in your background—whether it be science, medicine, art, music, or simply being a great friend—with what you've experienced and know to be true in your spirit and heart. You will be accompanied in your efforts by the universe rejoicing that there is someone who can both listen and act. When your inner experience is strong, you can draw upon it to act.

An experience of Unity by Judith Simpson:

> *There is complete interconnectivity at all levels of perception: the mind, the emotions, the body, the personality. What is 'mine?' Why does it even matter that 'I' differentiate myself? The very thought separates me from Reality. This is the true surrender—the surrender of one's exaggerated sense of one's individuality. So difficult, so necessary, so much the subject/object of our remembrance.*

In my own experience this awareness dawned gradually. It wasn't the 'Big Bang.' I had experienced a whiff of this state at times on retreat or at seminars. There had been a gradual destabilization of my 'edges.' I felt it happening, but didn't know how to interpret it. I had no idea that it presaged such an intense, and at times terrifying, awakening. I actually felt like a failure, that I couldn't manage this grace. I had to learn to live in it without being 'out of it.' I had to connect my realization with my history, my emotions, and my physicality. Except at the time, I didn't understand any of this. How strange, in retrospect, that the state of unity I had desired was one that, in the day to day, I interpreted as distance from God. Truly, the Beloved plays hide-and-seek with the lover.

The 'Look' of Step Seven

In the East, an ancient story is told of a wall of mystery around a garden in a village. Whenever anyone tried to climb up the wall to look at the other side, he or she would smile and jump over the wall, never to return. Understandably, the people of that country became very curious to know what mystery lay behind that wall. They thought they would arrange something that would pull the person back so that he could glimpse the other side, but would be forced to return to talk about what he saw.

When the next person tried to climb over the wall, curious to see what was on the other side, the people who saw him climb put chains on his feet and held him so that he would not go over. When he looked at the other side, he, too, was delighted with what he saw and smiled. Those who held the chains to pull him back found, to their great disappointment, that once he had been pulled back to earth, he had lost his powers of speech. Such is the intensity of the transformation in Step Seven.

If you are unsure about whether you have made your way into Step Seven or are in Step Five, you're in Step Five. Step Six is an unmistakable surrender; the third, fifth and seventh steps are exuberant; but only the seventh step has the beauty of having been through the sixth step.

We have found, when sitting in meditation with a person who has made this seventh step of face-to-face experience of Reality, that it leaves a distinct impression upon that person's actual physical face. It comes through as a sort of pressure upon one's own face. Something about feeling the radiance of the One upon your face creates this energetic shining-out, which can be felt by others. The Step Five expert has his say, but the one who has the real knowing of Step Seven tends to listen and smile a lot.

The Student Becomes the Teacher

The classical Sufi term for Step Seven, *Talib,* means "seeker," but it is the qualification to be a real teacher. We say that a teacher is someone who has fully learned how to be a student. Though you may need to learn the skills and techniques of effective communication, you now possess a deeper foundation that allows you to teach those who aspire to unity.

The reason is that *all that you have learned through your life is now completely generalizable.* In business life, this step makes a leader of an industry into a statesman. You may have been a physicist; now you write love poetry. You may have been a CEO; now you are addressing the development of the third world, or ecology, or what gives people meaning. The Expert (Step Five) tries to do these things also, but their ideas don't work; they fail to take into account the different ideals people have, the different types of people, and their different attitudes. At Step Five, you cannot see beyond the way that has worked for you, and so that's all you can really promote.

Ironically, you don't feel much like an expert at Step Seven. The surrender of Step Six has removed your self-assertion. In a state of awe and wonder, life seems bewildering; you're amazed at the beauty you had missed before and the immense vastness of the inner world. But this emotion is what makes you a good teacher.

Reflections on Step Seven

Following meditation, please reflect upon these questions:

Have you had a mystical experience: a direct experience of the universe without an observer? What did it feel like?

Have you experienced, without feeling fear or resistance, a Presence that dissolved you? When did it happen, and how did it feel?

Have you had an experience of Oneness that lasted a day or more?

Have you had a period of bewilderment in which you couldn't speak?

Chapter 17
Step 8: Guidance

GOD SPEAKS TO EVERYONE, not only to the messengers and teachers. God speaks to the ears of every heart, but it is not every heart which hears it. God's voice is louder than the thunder, and God's light is clearer than the sun – if one could only see it, if one could only hear it. In order to see it and in order to hear it a person should remove this wall, this barrier which (s)he has made of the self. Then (s)he becomes the flute upon which the divine Player may play the music of Orpheus which can charm even the hearts of stone. – HIK[64]

In the eighth initiation, you communicate with God, so that God becomes to you a living entity; God is then no longer an ideal or an imagination, no longer one whom you have made; the One whom you once made has now become alive – a living God. Before this there was belief in God, there was worship of God; perhaps God was

[64] Hazrat Inayat Khan, Vol. 14, The Smiling Forehead, The Symbol of the Cross

> made in the imagination; but in this stage God becomes living. And what a phenomenon this is! This stage is a miracle in itself.
>
> The God-realized person need not speak of or discuss the name of God; your presence will inspire the sense of God in every being, and charge the atmosphere with it. Everyone that meets you, whether spiritual or moral or religious or without religion, will feel God in some form or other. – HIK[65]

Communication

The Presence you felt in Step Seven now becomes so real and available to you that you can dialogue with It. The lights and sounds, images and voices you experienced in meditation, now part of your everyday reality, become the experience of an omnipresent, all-pervading Being with which you can communicate.

At Step Seven, you might have called the Presence you felt, an energy, or "The Force," but that would not feel right in Step Eight. It is clear now that you are a being, communicating with a Being. The essential nature of self and the universe is the same; both are beings. If the nature of self were different from the nature of the universe, then how could the self belong to the universe, and ever aspire to unity? This realization opens the possibility for each being to share the insight, wisdom and desire of the other, and indeed this is what occurs.

> It is after feeling the presence of God and after being in communication with God that we come to realize God. When you can touch God in everybody, then God tells

[65] Hazrat Inayat Khan, Vol. 10, The Path of Initiation and Discipleship, 1. The Path of Initiation

> you about God's Self, because God sees you have no hate, no prejudice. You have seen your Beloved, and your Beloved tells you all.
>
> The saints and sages, who have been gifted with insight, often commune with God through their inner heart-development. In meditation, one is consulting with God, feeling God. This does not mean that one has a special meditation for every little problem. Keeping fixed periods for communion with God, establishing rhythms, and devoting the whole heart to God at those times helps more than anything else.
>
> Early morning meditations are especially valuable for consulting with God and receiving help. Gradually, this spiritual communion will become such a power, such a reality, that it will continue day and night. The heart will open and the intuition tells one how to act, when to move, to travel, to marry, to make any important change in life, or even to meditate or perform extra spiritual deeds. In this condition, gradually all of life takes on a grand unity. [66]

Now that you have found The Living Being within your heart, you come to rely upon that Being. Your being has conversations with Being. What decision would you make now without consulting the Being within your heart? None.

The name that Hazrat Inayat Khan gave to this initiation is *Mureed*, meaning "Disciple." Why should the step of the Disciple come after the step of the Teacher? The Disciple contains the universe that the Teacher has discovered. The Disciple knows that the teacher is within, so there is no need for the teacher to reveal something; there is nothing to ex-

[66] Hazrat Inayat Khan, Vol. 10, The Path of Initiation and Discipleship, 1. The Path of Initiation, 8th Initiation

plain. Everything is being revealed to the Disciple from within, as the heart answers every question put to it.

Making Decisions

The indication of this step is in the way you make decisions.

- At Step Three, you made decisions by analyzing the facts to consider which direction gave you an advantage.
- At Step Four, you decided every question by holding it up against the light of your ideal, whether practical or not.
- At Step Five, you learned to be very effective by harnessing the power of your heart so you could attain your ideal.
- At Step Six, you passively allowed your ideal to work in your life without needing to understand it.
- At Step Seven, realizing that your ideal is only the ideal of one person, you became aware that reality has its own design. That is, the Universal Heart is creating desire within all hearts to fulfill its own wish.
- Now, at the eighth step, you make decisions by asking the Universal Heart within your heart what It wants.

The guidance is clear and unequivocal, and you can follow the answers you receive with complete confidence. Consequently, you experience a very rare combination of detachment *and* conviction. You do not do that which is personally motivated, but that which you are *led* to do.

At Step Eight, you are capable of making decisions that seem to be to your disadvantage. In fact, you will be tested by receiving guidance which will be very difficult to follow. But you know that the Being in your heart would never guide you wrongly, and anyway you always see the gain in the loss and the loss in the gain. Clearly, there is no other way of making decisions that produces better results, and no greater way of living than in the presence of Guidance.

> Then there is a third stage: as the soul evolves further a person begins to see reason behind reason. So (s)he sees several reasons, one hidden behind the other. There is a reason for everything, whether agreeable or disagreeable, right or wrong. [67]

If you seem to have a loss by following your guidance, there is a gain as well, for there is a gain in every loss and a loss in every gain. The purpose of some intuition is to test your faith in your intuition. Eventually, you come to see that there is no other way of making decisions that produces better results, and no greater way of living than in the presence of the One Heart's guidance.

Now that you have found The Living Being within your heart, you come to rely upon that Being. Your being has conversations with Being. You would make no decision now without consulting the Being within your heart. Where would you want to go in your life? Wherever makes the feeling of the pleasure of Being stronger.

The Role of the Teacher in Step 8

Still, the Disciple needs a living teacher to check the intuitions that are coming from within, and to guide him/her on to the next step. This person is the teacher-of-teachers, who has attained Stage Four, Step Twelve. In Sufi terminol-

---

[67] Hazrat Inayat Khan, Vol. 14, The Smiling Forehead, The Process of Spiritual Unfoldment, Stages of the Path

ogy, this position is called *Pir-o-Murshid,* or simply *Pir,* which literally means, "The Elder of the Masters." Practically, the training of a Disciple may be turned over to a *Shaikh,* which means a representative of the Pir-o-Murshid, who has attained steps ten or eleven.

> Of course, one has one's spiritual teacher, his shaikh, near at hand, who may and often must be consulted when doubt arises. The spiritual teacher can best help the student when the student looks upon the teacher as a link on the chain which connects the student to God.[68]

The Pir-o-Murshid's role in the spiritual life of the disciple is to:

- Help you discriminate between the voice of your heart and all other voices .
- Encourage you to follow your heart's lead, no matter the obstacles.
- Point out the expansion of choices and opportunities you now have, which you might not have noticed.
- Hold up the mirror in which you can see both the divine and the limited parts of yourself, so you can overwhelm the second with the first. Because you have discovered your pure Being, you are quite willing to dis-identify with your limited being. It's like giving a stone to get a pearl; you just need to notice where that trade is being asked of you.
- Demonstrate and model "The Manner," the character you are developing, which will be demonstrated in Step Nine.

> One reaches the door of Rasul [The Christ Consciousness] through Shaikh, the spiritual guide [and represen-

[68] Hazrat Inayat Khan, Githas, Meditation, 8, Communing with God

> tative of the Pir-o-Murshid], whose soul owing to devotion is focused on the spirit of Rasul and so is impressed with the divine qualities. The friendship with Shaikh has no other motive than guidance in seeking God. As long as your individuality lasts it will last, as long as you are seeking God it will last, as long as a guidance is needed it will last. The friendship with Shaikh then merges into the friendship with Rasul.
>
> A mureed [student], by devotion to the Pir-o-Murshid, learns the manner of love, standing with childlike humility, seeing in the face of every being on earth his Pir's blessed image reflected.[69]

The Surrender of Step 8

This step requires a short surrender (down and to the left) which symbolizes a change in one's self-concept, followed by a long journey in the heart. It leads to a point near the beginning but on the right side, indicating a surrender of the heart. The mind is now convinced that its place is in service to the heart, and the heart is receptive to the guidance of the Universal Heart. (See Figure 2)

Step Eight, an even-numbered step, is a step in surrender, similar to the surrender of Step Six, but whereas in Step Six you didn't have a solution in view, now you have the solution with you at all times. Then, the challenge was to have faith that the universe would eventually respond to you. Now, the challenge is to integrate the guidance of the universe which is filling your heart, with your own ideas and desires. This is done not by negotiation, but by surrender. You come to realize that the guidance of your heart is

---

[69] Hazrat Inayat Khan, Vol. 5, Love, Human and Divine, 6. Divine Love

your own desire, even if it isn't what your mind had imagined.

> Right attitude towards God is a direct response to God. For His voice is continually coming as an answer to every call. The ears of the heart should be open and focused on that source whence the voice is coming. When that is done then the teacher within is found; then there is continual guidance, and one is guided to the extent that one keeps close to it. Then one needs no other guidance; but first the guidance of a spiritual teacher is necessary in order to come nearer to it.[70]

The great difficulty of Step Eight is that, in most cases, your life has to be completely rearranged to bring it in line with your heart's guidance. When the Heart begins to speak, it becomes clear that your life has so far demonstrated a different priority than that of preparing for and accomplishing your purpose. Some of your deepest wishes, that would have prepared you for your mission, have been denied or overridden while you have spent most of your time on diversions. Without the clear guidance of your heart, surrounded by stimulation and feeling the need to please others, one naturally goes astray. The realization of having gone astray was never so strong before; it requires a personal, direct, undeniable sense of the "right" way in order to see the difference from your usual way. Until now, what is "right" has been defined by others, or by some idealistic and unattainable notion. Now the heart's guidance is ever present and undeniable, and it demands that your life align to it.

The realignment of your life will happen in this step,

---

[70] Hazrat Inayat Khan, Vol. 6, The Alchemy of Happiness, The Secret of Life, Attitude towards friends

either dramatically or gently. When it happens dramatically, it's like a death and rebirth. If it happens gently, it's like a falling away of old interests and friendships that are replaced by new ones. Now that your heart can set your direction, most of the things you did when you were seeking direction become uninteresting. What is life to an ordinary person is like death to the mystic, and what is death to the mystic is life to the ordinary person.

You are preparing for Step Nine. You'll find you can make deep and profound psychological changes and take an active part in the rebuilding of your psyche. This transformation is performed by the pull of the attractiveness of your emerging personality, rather than by the push of disgust with what you have allowed yourself to become. Consequently, it is a process of love, with harmony and beauty emerging more and more. You may be acutely aware of the lack of harmony in your personality, but your love for beauty will bring out beauty.

Guidance and Intuition

Intuition is a common experience whereby the conscious mind receives a message from the unconscious. Guidance is delivered by intuition, but not all intuition is guidance. Even if your intuition is very good, it does not indicate necessarily that you've attained the eighth step of realization. The challenge of discriminating between guidance, other intuition, desires and whims is difficult enough for you at Step Eight; it is not possible at all at an earlier step. Everyone receives messages intuitively, but the question is, "Who is speaking, and who is listening?"

Who is speaking? It is fascinating to observe the frequent occurrences of serendipity, coincidence and synchronicity.

Such things are always happening — this is the magnetism of the heart at work — and your heart is pleased to be noticed. Whether they realize it or not, everyone is in constant dialogue with their environment; even the rocks and trees have something to say. You are living in a sea of voices — the wind in the trees, the gurgling brook, the words of a child, the song on the radio — and at night you're immersed in the images and words of your dreams. In truth, there is only One Who is Speaking, the Spirit of Guidance, Who uses all these channels to deliver Its Message, superimposed over each voice and the echoes of your own thoughts and desires.

Your thoughts echo in the dome-like space around you, to come back to your ears through the voices of others. People around you will say things that you've been thinking and feeling. Psychics are skilled at providing this sounding-board; their words are echoes of your own conscious and unconscious thoughts. Events will occur that your heart has attracted in accordance with its desires. Many are misled by signs that reflect their inner confusion and miss the signs that point the way home.

Who is listening? Without the realization of unity at Step Eight, a person will hear the voices and observe the events of their life without getting the message they carry. It requires realization, which comes from inner experience, to benefit from intuition. A mystic at Step Eight is guided by many signals and signs—in the tea leaves and in the stars they see the message written by the Hand of God; in the voice of a stranger and the expression of their friend they hear the Voice of God. The message falls upon their open heart and is interpreted in the light of their realization, so the meaning a mystic receives may be very different from the meaning others would see or hear.

Susanna gave us an example of correctly interpreting her intuition as guidance:

I had a very bad cough for a period of many months. Nothing I did could relieve it. Although I did go to doctors, who were unable to cure me, I knew that the cough was not really a physical illness but the harbinger of a great inner change that was coming. My interpretation of the symptoms was lost on my friends, who thought the cause of my cough must be in the past, not in the future.

Seeking a healer, I went to a seminar, and there was my future teacher. I recognized him at once, and immediately had an intense coughing fit such that I had to leave the room. It was as if the coughing signal had to exclaim, "He is the one I've been telling you about all this time!" My friends thought my coughing attack was a bad sign, but I knew it marked the goal of my spiritual search. After I took initiation, my cough disappeared altogether.

Other stories of guidance come from our students:

The key to authentic guidance for me is about what's in the process of becoming. It's not as if the impetus does not already exist, in reality. It's catching the wave, so to speak, of what is already becoming on this plane of existence; what is manifesting, coming into being, at the moment; and being able to articulate what that direction is. In many ways I've found that the root of guidance is participation in the intelligence behind the Universe, the mind of God if we anthropomorphize the Divine Being, and then literally speaking or acting upon what that is. In Step Eight we are passive to the influence of the Divine Being, as is the crescent moon. The guidance we receive is given in relationship to the completeness of our surrender of self. There is a saying that's popular now, that we "trust our guidance." However, in my experience with this stage, trusting my *guidance is a misnomer; one becomes not-I, and then one is guided.*

❁

The specific signal I get is that the internal sound I hear, what some call the "music of the spheres," gets very loud, very insistent, a real pest at times, to the point where I just want it to tone down . . . but then I realize that something's coming through. Sometimes it just comes out, verbally, and I wonder where in the world that *came from, but then I 'hear' this intense ringing sound, very loudly, and I understand that I am catching the wave from nonexistence into existence and I should halt my mental constructs and pay attention.*

❁

For me the 'click' is when I get some inspiration and am absolutely enthralled with it, obsessed by it, wild horses wouldn't keep me from it. I know it's right; it lives in my awareness night and day. Of course, it's generally the guidance I need to take the next step, and that guidance is replaced with another divine obsession, and so on. But that's how we progress, how guidance manifests in/through us. Now I more or less know it when I feel it! (And conversely, I know when something's over, too.)

❁

I may not be really in tune with my voice of guidance. Sometimes I get the feeling I may actually be ignoring it because I want to do my own thing. This could explain why I sometimes look back and realize missed opportunities and why I sometimes ask myself, "How did I get into this mess?" It may relate to some reluctance to really go deep and find my purpose in life.

In Step Eight, your meditations often become dialogues with that spirit that creates you anew on every inhalation, and through love sustains and guides you to further realization. As these dialogues develop, they become increasingly clear, less metaphorical or symbolic and more literal. If this guidance is ignored, or overridden, then the Spirit of Guidance will have to take some other form to deliver its message, eventually reverting to illness or tragedy to get your attention. We are always given the message most gently at first.

When you need guidance in your life, the best process is the private, spiritual retreat which allows for uninterrupted meditation of several days or weeks.

Reflections on Step Eight

After meditation, write about this step in your journal. You might start with the following questions:

> What are some of your experiences of intuition that gave you non-logical information about the world or yourself?
>
> What experience have you had that you feel was guidance for your development?
>
> Did you confirm your guidance with a teacher or insightful friend?

Chapter 18

Step 9: Illumination

Thy light hath illuminated the dark chambers of my mind;
Thy love is rooted in the depths of my heart;
Thine own eyes are the light of my soul;
Thy power worketh behind my action;
Thy peace alone is my life's repose;
Thy will is behind my every impulse;
Thy voice is audible in the words I speak;
Thine own image is my countenance.
My body is but a cover over Thy soul;
My life is Thy very breath, my Beloved, and
My self is Thine own being. – HIK[71]

Love alone illuminates the heart.
The heart is in the center of the being.
When it is illumined the whole being becomes light;
when it is dark the whole being is in darkness.
The soul has its light, because the soul is light,
but it cannot give its light to the external being
if the heart that is between them is darkened,
nor can the body give its experiences to the soul. – HIK[72]

THE INNER LIGHT WHICH YOU DISCOVERED in Step Seven, and which you communicated with in Step Eight, has been integrated into your self-concept in Step

[71] Hazrat Inayat Khan, Sayings, Gayan, Ragas

[72] Hazrat Inayat Khan, Vol. 14, The Smiling Forehead, The Four Paths, Devotion

Nine. By claiming the light you become a lamp, a lamp that shines light into the world from your heart. This is illumination: the uncovering of the divine spark within.

An illuminated heart radiates light like a torch in the darkness, lighting your way to the fulfillment of your purpose and harmonizing the world to the rhythm of your heart. The clouds of doubt and fear are scattered by the inner light that dispels confusion and brings continual hope.

Illumination is also the completion of your individuality as a unique expression of the One Being. This is shown in your ability to dedicate yourself to the purpose of your life, accomplish your heart's wish, fulfill your obligations, recognize the divine in everyone, forgive and appreciate everyone in your life, and have no blame of anyone for anything.

Illumination is attainable by everyone, and illumination is the longing of every heart. Yet few people experience illumination in their lifetime because it requires training with a teacher. If one wants to become an opera singer, a marathon runner, a medical doctor or an astrophysicist, one expects to go to school and take instruction from a qualified teacher of that field, yet with that ultimate art form and most challenging project, the development of personality and wisdom, people expect to find their own way. The one who can help people find their divinity and claim their spiritual inheritance is the one who can illuminate their being with his or her heart.

Step Nine was called *The Sufi* by Hazrat Inayat Khan. The meaning of Sufi is "wise."

> When the Seeker [Step 7] becomes responsive, then (s)he is a Disciple [Step 8]. When (s)he has assimilated the teaching and begins to show it, then (s)he becomes a Sufi

[Step 9].
–HIK[73]

The eighth step, Guidance, which is essential for a disciple, is even-numbered, representing the left foot, which is receptive, as needed for assimilation. The ninth step is with the right foot, which is active, so in this step you *show* the teaching.

Completing the Personality

At the ninth step, you have fulfilled the commitment to spiritual development that you made at the first step. You began the path to explore yourself and uncover all that had been covered. The aim of the work through nine steps is the completion of the human personality, the greatest possible work of art. This art requires not only knowing yourself the way you have developed in life, which occurs at Step Five, but knowing the potentials in yourself that are glimpsed in the unraveling of yourself in Step Six, and revealed in the One Reality experienced in Step Seven.

The ninth step in realization is necessary to complete your personality; your personality is like a painting and this realization is like the vision of the artist. At this point, you have visualized the whole picture and outlined all its parts: the foreground, the background, the color scheme, and the emotion have all been set. To make this painting into a work of art there is still a tremendous effort required. All the parts of the painting must work together in harmony. The theme must be implemented in every detail. The effect of the painting upon the viewer must be considered. The result, as in life, is integrity, where the being is whole.

---

[73] Hazrat Inayat Khan, Sangitha 2, Ta'lim, Testing a Pupil

Without the realization of the Sufi, the personality cannot be finished. It would be like trying to perfect each aspect of a painting without having an overall design. You are now qualified as an artist of being, but you must still perfect your technique and apply the effort. Then your personality will be a beautiful work of art, your gift to others and your offering to God.

Finishing the art work of the personality has also been called "polishing the heart." This uses an ancient Sufi metaphor of the heart as a mirror. The earliest mirrors were polished metal, before glass mirrors were invented. The metal surface was quite reflective, but required constant polishing or else rust would develop. Only if the mirror was not rusty could a person see themselves in its reflection. This metaphor shows an objective of the illuminated heart: that all other hearts would be able to find themselves in that heart. Practically, it means that others are able to see their own ideal in you. The mirror-like quality of heart is also reflective of the divine light; the light that appears in the heart at Step Nine is actually a reflected light. All hearts reflect the light of the spiritual sun, and in Step Nine, the reflector has been polished.

At this step all complaints cease. There is no one who has not been forgiven; there are no resentments left. All the wounds are healed, to the extent that they will no longer drive your actions. There is no blame toward anyone for anything. Your personality becomes your artwork and when any imperfections are found, you immediately tend to their repair, grateful for the opportunity to improve.

Your contentment is great; you love meditation and worship, and practice both continually. Your gratitude for your spiritual school is such that the mention of your school or teacher can bring tears to your eyes. You can easily commune with nature and find unity, with your eyes open or shut. Life is not a struggle because you live in the guidance and blessing of the Universal Heart. The harmony and peace of this life is impossible to imagine, like a fairy tale, to one who has not made this step in realization. Of course, you still have aspirations and challenges, and they can cause agitation and stress when you choose to pursue them. But you also have indifference and an undefeatable joy. If you had to die tomorrow, you would be ready. Whenever you meditate, you are whole, and you can meditate whenever and for as often as you wish. You can hold the attunement of meditation throughout your day; you can also drop it, and you can get it back again in a moment.

In the path of the heart, it is important to fulfill our desires because they point us toward our purpose. But what really is your desire? At an earlier step, people are quick to say what they want, but they're not often right. If they get what they want, perhaps they'll wish they didn't; or if they don't get what they want, perhaps they'll be glad they didn't. A person's perception of what they want is often an expression of the past, not the future. Now, no desire seems as compelling as the wish to make the contribution you are given to make. When you identify this wish, you have identified the divine will operating as your own.

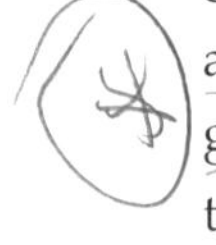

Like the other odd-numbered steps before, this is a step in power and glory. Here you have completed the sequence of Concentration, Contemplation and Meditation. The special state that is gained was called by Pir Vilayat Inayat Khan, "Being passive with respect to the divine action upon you," a synthesis of initiative and responsiveness that he

called "passive-volition."

The Manner of God

The ninth initiation is called *Akhlak-e-Allah*, which means the Manner of God. The one who touches that realization expresses in their manner the manner of God; their outlook on life is God's outlook; their action, thought, and word are God's action, thought, and word.[74]

The Sufi recognizes the divine in all beings of the world, and is ready to learn from young and old, educated and uneducated, rich and poor, without questioning from whom (s)he learns. Then the Sufi begins to see the torch of truth which shines before them in every being and thing in the universe. Thus the Sufi sees the vision of God, the worshipped deity, in immanence, manifest in nature, and life now becomes for them a perfect revelation both within and without.[75]

You have become "the one who knows that he knows." Your manner would never reveal this; the Sufi is humble towards all. There is no need to impress another, or diminish another to gain advantage, since God has revealed God's own Being within the Sufi, and the world has nothing to add to this greatness.

The Message of our time is the awakening of the consciousness of humanity to the divinity of the human being.[76]

This awakening has occurred in you. At this step you have all the parts of your being in place. You have not only

---

[74] Hazrat Inayat Khan, Vol. 10, The Path of Initiation and Discipleship, 1. The Path of Initiation

[75] Hazrat Inayat Khan

[76] Hazrat Inayat Khan

seen the divinity within, you have found a channel of reliable communication with it, and you can rest comfortably in the confidence of your inner reality.

This is a place of ultimate freedom and ease in recognizing and living one's true purpose. And although it is a completion of sorts, it is only the beginning of a whole new way of being that will continue to evolve – a dynamic equilibrium rather than a stasis.

Examples of Step Nine

Judith Simpson wrote beautifully about this in her contribution:

I've come to think of this step as the step of satisfaction. It's being able to live from *(not 'in,' which is, I think, Step Seven) the awareness of the Divine. It is not we who are satisfied with God or with our lives; rather, it is God being aware of having fully manifested in and through us, being satisfied with Himself, his perfection, through us. Yes, we continue to struggle against our limitations—which we experience even more acutely because we feel intensely the extent to which they limit our ability to express what is constantly coming through. It's the wish of God that we experience and fulfill our destiny, which is happiness.*

Personally, I've found this stage to be evolutionary. It's important not to confuse completeness with being static. At any/every moment the Being of God is complete, but evolving. When I am in the state of satisfaction, or completeness, it lasts for a while, but then another octave of completeness presents itself, to which I aspire. That's how I've experienced this: there is an overall recognition or acknowledgement of what is perfect in the now, but the now never lasts forever and one is impelled towards an even more 'tuned' level of satisfaction. The Being of God is constantly discovering Him/Herself anew through us, if we do not inhibit the action of God on/in/through ourselves. Each time I hold my breath in participation with the Heart of Oneness, I must be re-breathed anew. Each breath is an opportunity to re-adjust to completeness. Nothing is complete for more than a breath because of the very nature of the Intelligence behind all existence.

As Judith so eloquently writes, living life in an awakened, self-realized state is a continual unfolding, not a place of rest. The rewards of practicing this kind of living are many: those things that can seem overwhelmingly important to a less awakened person don't perturb you when you've come into Step Nine. That which confuses people who are not yet at this point on the Map won't seem at all confusing to you; and what may seem frightening, even horrifying, to others won't have these effects on you. You won't fear disappointment or failure, and when these happen, your courage and hope will remain unaffected. You become noble and content.

Loving Your Life

> The necessity in the spiritual path is the loving of the everyday life. There are no strict morals which a spiritual guide enforces upon a person, for that work has been given to the outward religions. It is to the exoteric side of spiritual work that the outer morals belong, but the essence of morals is practiced by those treading the spiritual path.
>
> 1. Their first moral principle is constantly to avoid hurting the feeling of another.
> 2. The second principle is to avoid allowing themselves to be affected by the constantly jarring influences which every soul has to meet in life.

3. The third principle is to keep their balance under all different situations and conditions which upset this tranquil state of mind.
4. The fourth principle is to love unceasingly all those who deserve love, and to give to the undeserving their forgiveness; and this is continually practiced by them.
5. The fifth principle is detachment amidst the crowd; but by detachment I do not mean separation. By detachment is only meant rising above those bondages which bind one and keep one back from the journey towards the goal. — HIK[77]

Reflections on Step Nine

Again, return to meditation. Then consider:

Can you say you have no regrets, no resentment and no blame of anyone for anything?

Are there any experiences in your life for which you are not thankful?

[77] Hazrat Inayat Khan, Vol. 1, The Inner Life, Attaining the Inner Life, 5. Loving Life

Chapter 19

The Steps of Relationship

AN UNDERSTANDING OF THE MAP is a powerful tool in navigating relationships and in understanding their progressions, regressions, difficulties and joys. To refine the use of this tool, let's look at the Steps in a slightly different way, tailored to clearly describe aspects of relating in an intimate relationship:

1. *Commitment*: Here, you take a step in a specific direction without knowing the outcome. You establish a specific intention as you initiate a relationship or a deepening of the relationship. Re-commitment is needed after a challenge or change in circumstances.

2. *Testing*: The testing phase measures the boundaries of the relationship. Here, one partner tests the other's willingness to limit his or her freedom, in some way, for love.

3. *Harmony*: Understanding is developed and tolerance and forgiveness grow, creating a stable relationship in which communication is good, understanding matures, and

harmony is developed.

4. *Idealization*: In the Step of Idealization, beauty becomes the object of each partner's pursuit. Adoration develops for the one in whom you see your ideal. Love comes from the heart, not the mind, so you can't list the reasons for your love; love is all-consuming, and doesn't depend on being returned.
5. *Expertise*: In this step, you become an expert in relationships. By seeing the ideal in your partner and by applying the power of your heart to that ideal, you can bring out the best in the other. This is the culmination of all the previous steps of love: your love provides what the beloved needs for growth. You take responsibility for inspiring and facilitating the personal growth of the other people in your life, rather than expecting them to be able to live according to your ideal of them.
6. *Unlearning*: You realize here that you know nothing about your partner – he or she is incomprehensibly greater than you thought before. Instead of "helping" your beloved, all you can do is serve him or her as their needs require, for their inner knowledge is guiding them in ways you can't understand. Love is not about pleasure or fun, but about longing, perseverance, hope, patience, and willing sacrifice and surrender – as love teaches you to say, "Thou, not I."
7. *Union*: Realizing that all that you love in the other is the same as that which you love in yourself, and furthermore, the One Who Loves others through you also loves you through others, you begin to love everyone as you love yourself. This shortening of the Golden Rule has profound implications: it leads you to seeing every hu-

man relationship as a way of practicing your relationship with God.

Startled by the vision of the divine in the other, your relationship becomes a spiritual path to the divine Beloved. Spiritual fulfillment becomes a main purpose of the relationship, and both partners dedicate themselves and the relationship to developing a greater realization of the unity of being. As you become more able to merge in intimacy with other human beings, you move closer to a non-dual relationship with God.

8. *Guidance*: Everyone needs feedback to evolve, yet seldom do people like to be told what to do. In the Step Eight relationship, you hear your partner's voice as the Spirit of Guidance, accepting it without resistance, realizing that God is guiding and teaching you through your beloved. There is a Jewish teaching that after marriage, God hears the prayer from either partner as the prayer of both. This is an extension of the dialogue that occurs in Step Eight between individual beings and the Universal Being.

9. *Illumination*: To be with your beloved is to be more yourself than you can be by yourself. There is no blame of the other, or any one, for anything. Between you, there are no barriers, no possessiveness, no assertiveness. The sense of purpose is so strong for both of you that your relationship serves the Cause and the Cause serves your relationship.

Chapter 20
The Steps of Career

MANY PEOPLE ADVANCE IN REALIZATION as they pursue a career. Let's consider how the steps of realization look as you pursue career development.

1. *Commitment*: When you start a new job, or a new project, you start at Step One again. Become part of the team, accept a share of the effort and stress. Be aware that you cannot know what you've gotten into. The job may seem simple, but have hidden traps, or it may seem very difficult, but offer unseen help and advantages. There is a tendency to over-estimate your ability, which is not yet tested.

2. *Testing*: Demonstrate sacrifice and survive the challenges. Find your supporters and detractors. Be aware of the sacred cows and the monster nobody mentions.

3. *Harmony*: Adjusted to the job, you become competent, dependable, harmonious and well-liked. Boredom can set in at this point. You're very comfortable, but growth has stopped.

4. *Idealization*: Discovering an aspect of your personal ideal in your work, you find you're in the perfect job. Here you have the ability to attain your own goal of making a significant contribution to a significant organization. Aspire to excellence beyond the expectations of others. Turn away from what is conventional and similar to the competition. Beware of being uncompromising, unpractical or insolent.
5. *Expertise*: Apply your heart to becoming the best, irreplaceable, innovative, super-productive, star employee. Make your own job where you do what no one else can do. Follow your own ideal to a higher standard than the people around you or the company as a whole. Give yourself to your work without reservation, enthusiastically. Inspire and teach others; gain recognition from your industry. Beware of megalomania.
6. *Unlearning*: Challenge all your assumptions about business. Consider that everything you've learned is either wrong or inappropriate. Be humble. You will likely withdraw from leadership and become inner-directed. This is a good time for basic research. Consider: does the world really benefit from your work? Beware of cynicism.
7. *Unity*: Surprisingly, you see a bigger reason for being in this position than you ever imagined. You can serve the company indirectly, and your ideal, by contributing to something global of immense importance. The executive becomes a true leader, the scientist becomes a poet. Your greatness extends far beyond your own arena. Success becomes miraculous. You cannot fit your new vision into the old organization; basic restructuring is required. Be-

ware: the situation is highly dynamic; you must refresh your vision frequently.

8. *Guidance*: Your ability to communicate with the universe makes you aware of large-scale trends as well as personal guidance for yourself and the people around you. You are a seer, working on multiple levels, aware of opportunities that no one else sees. You take risks with confidence, and can change direction quickly. Be aware: you are a mysterious figure, respected and feared, a secret weapon for the company, but unpredictable.
9. *Illumination*: Your apparent job, its responsibilities and circumstances, is not important; there is only one job: awakening the consciousness of humanity to the divinity of the human being. In this job you are engaged every moment, and every time and place provides sufficient opportunity.

Chapter 21

Stage Four of Service

THE END AND SUM TOTAL OF ALL mysticism, philosophy, and meditation, of everything one learns and develops, is to be a better servant to humanity. Everything from the beginning to the end in the spiritual path is a training to be able to serve mankind better, and if one does not do it with that intention, one will find in the end that one has accomplished nothing.

There are many who seek wonder-working or great power to accomplish things. They may perhaps try and gain some power or other; but their soul will never be satisfied. The true satisfaction of the soul is in honest, humble service to another.

If there were two people before me, one with great power of wonder-working who could perform miracles, and another humble and kind and gentle and willing to do anything he could for his fellow-men, I would prefer

> this last man. I would say, the first is wonderful, but the other is a sage. — HIK[78]

The Map has described nine steps leading to the completion of the human psyche — to what end, for what purpose? Now we begin an additional nine steps in which the self is dedicated to the service of others, in expanding spheres of influence.

As one continues along the Map, the *real* self is awakened, and this self wants most to be a better servant to humanity—to offer one's self and all of its qualities of greatness—in humble, honest service to others. The person who can do this is a true mystic.

Dedicating One's Life to Service

Certainly, it would seem that any person who is living from the heart would wish to put their skills and energy into serving others. Every cause and organization wants your service, but who is being served?

> You're gonna have to serve somebody.
> Well, it may be the devil or it may be the Lord,
> But you're gonna have to serve somebody. – Bob Dylan[79]

The military uses the word "service"; so does the clergy. But are you serving the country or just the military, the congregants or just the church?

While we praise the ideal of service, we believe that each person should follow his or her own ideal of service. The aim is to re-commit to that mission for which you are destined and designed. That mission, the purpose of your life, is

---

[78] Hazrat Inayat Khan, Vol. 6, The Alchemy of Happiness, The Secret of Life, Attitude Towards Friends

[79] Bob Dylan, "Gotta Serve Somebody", from "Slow Train Coming"

absolutely unique. Beware anyone who claims to know what your mission is. It is helpful to have an ally, but you cannot fulfill your unique purpose by completely subsuming yourself into someone else's purpose.

If you will accept the idea that the aim of life is not happiness but growth and discovery, then you can accept that one life can end in tragedy and another in victory; one life can end with surrender and another can end with glorification. These are the steps of the progression of life, and your life can end at any point during this progression. Will your life end on the left foot or the right foot? Mahatma Gandhi was assassinated at the height of his power and his memory continues to lift people in all parts of the world. Vincent Van Gogh died in depression; now his paintings give the world joy.

We urge everyone to fully embrace every phase of life, anticipating that its progression will be a series of expansions and contractions, like breaths. At the end of a period of contraction, or surrender, one cannot remember the expansion and glory. And at the end of a period of expansion, one cannot remember the loss and grief of contraction. This too shall pass, and throughout all, we are never separate from the Universal Being.

We should not attempt to protect ourselves from the depth of despair in the feeling that we are not actually connected to anything beyond ourselves. Some use their faith in an ultimate and enduring connection as an insulation from their grief, but we wish to experience the full depth of grief, hopelessness and despair, unmitigated by any escapist belief. In allowing one's self to plummet to those depths, one allows grief to burn into glory.

The spiritual work in our time is not freedom and liberation; it is responsibility. In the second nine steps, the mystic becomes progressively more well-equipped to help other human beings to realize their own potentials and to join into meaningful work towards solutions to the world's many pressing problems. This kind of service to others can happen in so many ways. Every kind smile, gesture, or word—even every thought—has a helpful effect. But the more insight one has, the more one sees that people are hard to help.

It takes insight, tact and patience to guide a person toward the solution of their self-made problems. Most often, a person cannot be helped by giving him or her what he or she asks for. As Einstein said, "You cannot solve a problem in the same consciousness that created it." A person will ask for a bigger hammer to hit the wall that blocks their chosen direction, rather than for a map of the walls, a ladder, or a shovel.

Those who are willing to commit their lives to service naturally want to be as effective as possible. Many times a person of good will has an idea of how to help a person or a group of people—but does the willing helper have enough insight to see what's happening on the stage of life? Perhaps what they think is helpful is actually an impediment or interference. You can imagine a well-wishing person, moved by the plight of someone suffering in a play, rushing onto the stage to intervene. Would the playwright or the director, or even that actor who is being 'helped,' be grateful? The play may be ruined. You can easily see this on an individual level: many people who have a great power of concentration, dedication and courage are unable to act because they don't see clearly how to act or in what direction to move. Power is paralyzed without vision and unleashed in proportion to the confidence one has in the use of that power. This confidence comes to the mystic by Guidance, an intuitive voice that speaks in one's heart.

Those who have not had the experience of Unity can hardly imagine the coordination that exists between those who have. By definition, everyone who has experienced Unity has experienced the same thing. (The experience is interpreted differently, however, according to one's religion or culture.) The reality of this coordination among the mystics is so great that no one who knows of it would want to work individually. The ability to work as one coordinated body is very powerful, and this is the way the Representatives—men and women who have realized the second Nine Steps—work. The greater the power one is capable of handling, the more cautious one becomes with using it undirected.

With the completion of Step Nine, one has become truly useful. Such a person can work effectively, without a need to gather praise, avoid blame, or revenge a loss. There is no need and no blame; there is only, "Now, what can I do?" Most people who wish to be of service will find a wide variety of opportunities, for everywhere are causes pleading for your help. Once Step Nine has been attained, you can find a way to serve and to lead through projects that match your interests and skills. A few people will feel they want to coordinate their work, and those few are the ones who will take Step Ten.

Step Ten: The Khalif

> [After the] initiation called the Sufi [Step Nine], if one wishes to continue to help humanity, one is authorized

and initiated to work in that direction as a Khalif [the Representative]. — HIK[80]

Very few arrive at the tenth initiation in their lifetime, for after the first nine initiations begins what is called the phase of "self-realization." When after having gone through all the other stages of consciousness one arrives at this stage, one can speak very little; for it is beyond the stage of religion and even beyond the notion of God; it is the stage of *self-expression*. This stage of self-expression is reached when a person has thoroughly dug their self out, so that nothing of the self is left but only that divine substance; and only then is (s)he free to express him/her self.

Thus the tenth initiation is the awakening of the real self, the real ego, and this awakening is brought about by meditation, the meditation which makes one forget one's false or limited self. The more one is able to forget it, the more the real self awakens. — HIK[81]

After you have gone through the first three stages, the self has been so expanded that it becomes a container for the divine. Duality with God is experienced up through Step Six. Step Seven is the unity of self absorbed into God, which continues and develops through Step Nine. And then, miraculously, the self reappears, to take responsibility for the work that was given to your soul, the purpose of your life. This is the reason for the ego, and why it needs to be softened, but not annihilated.

The realization of Step Ten is that the best way to serve

---

[80] Hazrat Inayat Khan, Social Gathekas, 5. Different Schools of Sufism, The Sufi Order

[81] Hazrat Inayat Khan, Vol. 10, The Path of Initiation and Discipleship, 1. The Path of Initiation

others is to work in a coordinated way with those who have a planetary vision. Thus the surrender of Step Ten is to voluntarily set aside your own plans and priorities in order to assist the teacher in his/her way of working. This is another kind of sacrifice, performed to amplify the work of one who has a greater scope of responsibility, power and vision.

This notion may offend your sense of freedom and democracy. Freedom and democracy are great ideals for an individual, but those who devote themselves to service are not concerned with their personal freedom—love is attachment and responsibility is binding. Democracy and rule by consensus are not principles of the spiritual government, for these are structures that assume that all people have an equal ability. In service, there must be a meritocracy, a natural hierarchy based on ability. In any effective organization, and certainly in the spiritual government of the world, there is always a meritocracy, whether it is officially recognized by titles and job descriptions, or it is simply that people give more authority to those they trust more.

Imagine that you have volunteered for a disaster relief effort. There must be someone who has in mind the whole scope of the effort, who can therefor allocate resources and assign volunteers efficiently. These positions of leadership are not established by seniority, education or any favoritism. People who show more ability are immediately put into the position that best uses that ability. Those with self-mastery and the ability to inspire confidence in others quickly rise, whether they have prior experience of exactly this kind or not. A nurse doesn't try to do the work of a doctor—unless there is no doctor, in which case the nurse is effectively promoted to that position. The hierarchy is dynamic: one may assume a post and surrender it again.

It would be dangerous to take a higher position than one can handle, because each rank carries more responsibility. Therefore, there is no coveting of rank among those who serve. There are many cases of a person being damaged by trying to be what they are not ready to be. But progress is natural, and anyone who is willing to serve will be used to the fullest of their capacity.

Khalif means one who represents, or reflects, his or her living teacher. You realize at this step that the light which illuminates you is coming from the heart of your spiritual superior, reflected into your heart and from your heart.

Step Eleven: The Murshid

> In step eleven one experiences a sensation of splendor. It is like when a child is born and begins to see everything new: this old world is seen by the child as a new world. As soon as the point of view is changed by the help of meditation, one sees the whole world, which is before everybody and which everybody is seeing, quite differently.
>
> One begins to see reason behind reason, cause behind cause, and one's point of view also changes in regard to religion. It changes because where the average person would want to accuse or punish or blame a person for a certain action, the one who has risen to this stage can neither judge nor blame; (s)he only sees; but (s)he sees the cause behind the cause. Whom then shall (s)he accuse? Whom shall (s)he blame? How can (s)he refrain from forgiving, whatever be the fault, when (s)he sees all that is behind the fault, when (s)he sees the reason behind it, perhaps a more valid reason than even the one who committed the fault can see himself.
>
> Therefore naturally the manner of continually sacrificing, the manner of spontaneous love and sympathy, the

> manner of respect both for the wise and foolish, for the deserving and the undeserving, arises and expresses itself as divine life. It is at this stage that the human soul touches perfection and becomes divine, and that it fulfills its real purpose in life. — HIK[82]

Hazrat Inayat Khan called this step *Murshid,* which means "master." This word is not intended to have a gender bias; there are both female and male murshids. The murshid serves as a senior representative of the Pir. The splendor that you experience at this stage is due to the light of your heart, reflected from your spiritual superior, that you have now learned to direct where you wish. The ability to shine the light of your heart upon people, objects and situations is a great power that causes an immediate response in that which you illuminate.

Step Twelve: The Pir Among the Masters

The master who is willing to personally take on the responsibility for the spiritual evolution of a group of people is called the Pir of that spiritual community, which means "Elder." He or she reflects the light of the Source into the hearts of his or her representatives and students.

Every serious and sincere student must identify one living person who will accept the responsibility for guiding them to illumination and holding them safe through the path: that person is their Pir. The Pir might appoint a representative or a senior representative to conduct the specific training of the student, but the Pir retains the responsibility for the result.

---

[82] Hazrat Inayat Khan, Vol. 10, The Path of Initiation and Discipleship, 1. The Path of Initiation,

The Pir is the last station in the spiritual path that may be proclaimed; there are further steps but they are not claimed because it is unnecessary and such claims lead to challenge. The masters prefer to do their work quietly, with those who are attracted to them. Beyond that, those who need to know and have the inner experience necessary to know, will recognize each other and appreciate those who have an even greater capacity and responsibility.

More details are contained in the teaching of Hazrat Inayat Khan, and in retreats for advanced students.

Chapter 22
Internal Signs of Progress

FOR EVERY STEP IN THE PATH, there is an internal signal; by noticing these signals you can identify the corresponding realization. You may have passed these steps without noticing the internal signal, but you should be able to easily find the internal signal for the steps you have realized.

Step 1, Commitment: Buoyancy

Before you are able to commit to a person, a situation or a job, you go through an internal process of weighing the pros and cons, trying out in your mind, "Is this the right thing to commit myself to?" When you have made the commitment, it's a victory. You have taken a step toward the unknown, and that victory has an inner signal of buoyancy, joyousness and lightness.

Before you can still your mind to make this commitment you must still your body and nervous system. A remarkable sign of this is what we call the Monolithic Sensation. When you sit perfectly still for ten minutes or so, the pressure sensors in your flesh turn off, that is, they no longer send signals to the brain. It is by the sensation of pressure that you determine whether you are sitting or standing or laying down, whether your arms are resting on the legs or the arms of the chair, whether your back is straight or curved, etc. Since you have not moved and your position is unchanged, all your pressure sensors have been sending the same signals for several minutes. To conserve brain function, these signals just stop. It's similar to how you no longer hear a constant noise, or see a picture that has hung on your wall for years.

When your pressure sensors turn off, you'll feel like your body is made of one piece, indivisible. It is not numb, and you could move it if you try, but you have no inclination to move; you feel like a mountain. When you can sit still enough and long enough for this to happen, you have achieved a milestone in commitment, concentration and self-mastery.

Step 2, Testing: The Heartbeat Signal

A more difficult test of your concentration is to maintain focus through distraction. All you had to do to attain the Monolithic Sensation was to sit still, which showed a strong intention and commitment to the practice. But adding a distraction will test your concentration.

Your heartbeat is thumping in your chest every second or so, but you are not usually aware of it because there are so many other sensations to notice: visual and auditory sensations and also inner sensations like pain, discomfort, and breath. To feel your heartbeat you have to isolate this one sensation from among all the others, and hold it while the other sensations vie for attention.

You can build up to this by sensing your pulse in various parts of your body — wherever you look you should be able to feel your pulse there. Then look for that same rhythm in your chest.

Step 3, Harmony: Stable Breath Rhythm

Self-mastery is shown by your ability to maintain a breathing rhythm that is timed by your internal clock, your heartbeat. You have to coordinate active muscle control with an acute, passive sense of your heartbeat to achieve a rhythmic breath pattern. As you settle into this rhythm, you'll feel an integration of your body, mind and heart that is very pleasant, leaving you both relaxed and alert.

The Square Breath is chosen for your breath rhythm because it ensures that your breath is deep and full. As described in our earlier books, the rhythm is inhale for 6 heartbeats, hold your breath for 12 heartbeats, and exhale for 6 heartbeats.[83] But if you have a heart arrhythmia, skip the holding part. Your ability to take 10 Square Breaths in a row demonstrates your self-mastery, and also your trust because if fear would arise during the practice, it would demand more breath and interrupt your rhythm.

Step 4, Idealization: Pressure in Your Heart

You can get all the signals for Stage One, in the three steps above, without using your emotions. So the signals so far have been indications of mental power. In Step Four, you must use your emotion.

The signal for Step Four is a constant pressure in your chest that feels like your heart is expanding and pressing

[83] Described in *Living from the Heart*, pp 188-197, and *Energize Your Heart*, pp 226-231. See Bair and Bair (2007), (2010)

outward on your rib cage. It is actually the magnetic field of your heart that is expanding, which you will feel as pressure because you don't have a separate sensor for magnetism.

As your heart expands, with the pressure signal as your constant reminder, you can feel that your self is inside a large energy field. That's the sense that "I am inside my heart," the experience of Contemplation, the theme of Stage Two. This is not a mental conception; it is a deep, emotional experience that feels like a profound thankfulness.

This feeling of pressure in your heart is constant, not throbbing like the heartbeat, and it doesn't fade or hide like the heartbeat does. You can walk around with this sensation in your chest and when you do, you can be confident that your every word and action will express your ideal. Your internal censor and critic can be dismissed—you're in your heart and your heart is in charge.

Step 5, Expertise: Power in the Heart

A further step in the inner experience of the path is to feel yourself take on the identity of someone else. A shift in identity is the essence of Contemplation, and Contemplation requires the heart because only through love do you have access to the heart of another. The inner signal that you have accomplished contemplation is that you feel perfectly reasonable being the person you contemplate. If that person seems strange to you, you're not in their heart yet, for everyone feels reasonable to themselves.

Contemplating another person is practice for the great experience of becoming the One Who Is Peace, or the One Who Is Joy, etc. There are many faces of the One Being, and each of these faces expresses a different quality and emotion. The final signal of Step Five is the experience of calling upon the Being of Truth, for example, and then experiencing yourself as Truth. This is called invocation, and it is the way of using your heart to attract the qualities, emotions and energies that you choose, to augment yourself.[84] You invite by invocation a great being to live in your heart and express itself through you, to uncover an aspect of your own nature.

Step 6, Unlearning: The Inverted Space

The discovery of the "Inverted Space" is a key experience for Step Six. The Sufis teach that as you dive more deeply into yourself, you pass through an inverted space that reveals the universe within. That is, by feeling what is deeply personal, you discover the impersonal emotion of the universe. The Inverted Space is metaphysical, but has a physical analogue in the solar plexus, which the Sufis call the depth of the heart. The space within your heart is greater than the space of your body. It is like going through the mirror of the heart. The emotion you find there is bigger than your personal emotion, it is a cosmic emotion.

The signal for Step Six is an acute sense of a deep hole in your solar plexus. You may have reached the sixth step or beyond without noticing it, but if you are in Step Six and you send your attention into your solar plexus, you will find a deep well of emotion that is so strong and rich that it can't be described as any one emotion; it is all emotion simultaneously. It is both grief and elation. It is inconsolable suffering and incomparable bliss.

Your teacher can confirm your Step Six by noticing the inverted Space signal in his or her contemplation of you.

---

[84] Invocation is one of the Six Basic Powers, discussed in *Energize Your Heart*, p 105. See Bair and Bair (2007).

Step 7, Unity: Radiance in the Face

When you've faced the infinite light, as you do in Step Seven, it leaves an impression on your face. It is similar to the effect of facing the bright sun for an hour—the sun changes your face by leaving its impression on your skin. Even by just imagining a very bright light in front of you, you can feel the light exerting a faint pressure on your face. When your meditation becomes an experience of light, repeated regularly, your heart, mind, and even your body becomes transformed.

Your teacher, or anyone who has gone beyond the seventh step, can feel the light on your face; in contemplation of you they will feel light striking their own face, and light radiating from their face.

Step 8, Guidance: The Music of the Spheres

The eighth step is the experience of personal dialogue with the universe. An inner signal of this is the sensation of the "Music of the Spheres," the "Sound of Silence." When consciousness is vastly expanded, the senses also expand, resulting in sensations of sound, light, taste, smell and touch that are not physically stimulated. The auditory version of this expanded sensory experience is a ringing in the ears. When this sound is caused by a physical illness it is tinnitus, but when it can be deliberately turned on and off, it is a sign of cosmic consciousness spoken of by mystics as "flying on Garuda" (Hindu), or "riding Buraq" (Islam).[85] Johann S. Bach said he heard his symphonies in this inner sound.

Hazrat Inayat Khan taught that the inner sound is the

---

[85] For stories of Garuda which illustrate the fantastic nature of this experience metaphorically, see the Mahabharata. Smith (2009).

result of a vibration between the heart and head.[86] This is a meaningful metaphor for the dialogue between one's rational and intuitive self that occurs in Step Eight.

The first indication is the ability to hear the inner sound at some times during meditation. The second indication is to be able to hear the inner sound at will, without meditation. The third indication is to be able to hold the inner sound for as long as desired.

Other persons meditating with you will experience a louder inner sound in themselves. As J.S. Bach found, the inner sound has a complex variety. At first it seems like white noise, the sound of all sounds combined together, but as you listen to it, your own consciousness modulates the sound so that it conveys an impression, or even a message, to your mind. It is a wonderful stimulant to your intuition.

Step 9, Illumination: A Peaceful Atmosphere

What most people don't realize about peace is that peace is not a passive state; it is a great, radiant power. In the state of peace, your inner state is carried on an energy stream from your heart, on your exhalation, that reaches every person and object in your sphere of influence and brings all into the same state of peace.

The effect of this can be felt at once by anyone who has had the experience himself or herself. It is called "atmosphere," and it testifies to your realization. Your atmosphere is one characteristic of yourself that cannot be faked; it is created directly from your inner state.

Meditations

The signals described above are objective and verifiable

---

[86] Hazrat Inayat Khan, Sangitha I, Riyazat, Heart and Head

in others once you have experienced them yourself. The signal is an indication of the result of a spiritual practice, and there is a practice for each step of realization.

1. In the first stage, the stage of the mind, comprising the first three steps, we use various practices of Concentration. Much of what is taught publicly as meditation is actually concentration: practices of awareness, mindfulness, witness, or observation, are all concentration, in which you are aware of something else or some part of yourself, like your thoughts or emotions.
2. In the second stage, the stage of the heart, comprising steps four through six, the world is experienced through another point-of-view in Contemplation, where you become the object you concentrated upon. You may become the sun as your rays glance over the edge of the earth, or you may become the flower and feel what it's like to be admired for your beauty. You may become the other person and feel their heart and mind as your own. The essence of contemplation is a shift in identity to discover yourself in something or someone else.
3. In the Third Stage of spirit, there is no more observer. We call this the state of Meditation. Although we use the word meditation less formally to refer to our practice, the formal definition implies the state of unity.

All the steps of Concentration, Contemplation, and Meditation are taught in our school, the Institute for Applied Meditation (IAM), either as part of our curriculum of 24 courses, or as a comprehensive program in the University of the Heart.

Chapter 23
The Evidence of Progress

THE FOLLOWING QUOTATIONS are from Hazrat Inayat Khan, interspersed with our comments that relate his points to the nine steps of The Map. Note that these outer signs of progress lag behind the realization that makes them possible because it takes time to integrate the realization and express it naturally in one's attitude and behavior.

Inspiration

> There are innumerable outer signs of one's progress. What are these signs of progress?
>
> The first is that one feels **inspiration**, and that things which one could not understand yesterday are easy today.

Inspiration is the result of **Step Four**, the opening of the heart. The mind is never so bright as when the heart lights it up.

Power

The next sign of progress is that one begins to feel **power**. To some extent it may manifest physically and also mentally, and later the power may manifest in one's affairs in life. As spiritual pursuit is endless, so power has no end.

The experience of power is due to the application of your heart, as occurs in **Step Five**. The power of the heart is unfathomably greater than the power of the mind. The heart rules the body, providing not only circulation but also a co-ordinating rhythm. Energetically, the heart's magnetic field is a hundred times greater than the brain's magnetic field, and this magnetism is what creates attraction in a personality, charisma, and influence.

Happiness

The third sign of progress is that one begins to feel a **joy, a happiness.** But in spite of that feeling it is possible that clouds of depression and despair may come from without, and one might think at that moment that all the happiness and joy which one had gained spiritually was snatched away. But that is not so. If spiritual joy could be snatched away it would not be spiritual joy. It is not like material comforts; when these are taken away from us we have lost them; but spiritual joy is ours, it is our property; no death nor decay can take it away from us. Changing clouds like those which surround the sun, might surround our joy, but when they are scattered we will find our property still there in our own heart. It is something we can depend upon, something nobody can take away from us.

We have written about this joy with no reason that occurs in **Step Seven**. It is absolute joy because it comes from an inner experience, not an outer cause. This joy belongs to you because it is the joy of discovering your own soul of light.

Fearlessness

There is another sign of progress, and that is that one becomes **fearless**. Whatever be the situation in life, nothing seems to frighten one any more, even death. Then one becomes fearless in all that might seem frightening, and a brave spirit develops, a spirit which gives one patience and strength to struggle against all adverse conditions however terrible they seem to be. It can even develop to such an extent that one would like to fight with death. To such a person nothing seems so horrible that he would feel helpless before it.

To be fearless requires more than power and joy, it requires inner confidence that you will be able to make the right decision in every moment. In the realization of **Step Eight**, you feel guidance continuously, placing every footstep in the proper place. By tuning into your heart, you have a voice to warn and guard you, step-by-step, and with this constant reassurance you can be fearless, confident that you will be led to those opportunities that have been prepared for you, and not into a challenge greater than you can bear.

Peace

Still another sign of progress is that at times one begins to feel **peaceful**. This may increase so much that a restful feeling comes in the heart. One might be in the solitude, but even if one is in a crowd one still feels restful. Once peace is developed in a soul, that soul feels such a great power and has such a great influence upon those who approach it and upon all upsetting conditions and jarring influences coming from all sides, that just as water

> makes the dust settle down, so all jarring influences settle down under the feet of the peaceful.
>
> One may make the excuse that one's surroundings are worrying one, that one's friends are troublesome or that one's enemies are horrible; but nothing can withstand that peace which is awakened in the heart. All must calm down, all must settle down like dust after water has been sprinkled on it. — HIK[87]

Step Nine, Illumination, gives the experience of completeness, and supreme satisfaction. The degree of inner harmony and balance is so great that it feels as if lions would lie down at your feet.

---

[87] Hazrat Inayat Khan, Vol. 10, The Path of Initiation and Discipleship, 9. The Attitude of a Disciple

Chapter 24
The Culture of the Heart

BEHIND ALL THIS WORLD of various names and forms there is one life, there is one spirit. This spirit which is the soul of all beings is attracted towards unity, and it is the absence of this spirit which keeps the world unhappy. If you have just had some unpleasantness with your brother or sister, your food is tasteless, the night without sleep, the heart restless, the soul under a cloud. This shows that we do not necessarily live on food; our soul lives on love, the love that we receive and the love that we give. The absence of this is our unhappiness, and the presence of it is all we need. Nothing in the world is a greater healing power, a greater remedy, a greater happiness, than to be conscious of brotherhood and sisterhood and to be able to give that feeling to your child, master, neighbor, and friend. – HIK[88]

As we each develop our hearts individually, we have a collective effect upon the society as a whole. The heart of

---

[88] Hazrat Inayat Khan, Vol. 10, The Problem of the Day, 7. Brotherhood (1)

humanity is developed as people experience the One Heart in their own heart. And the breakthroughs occurring anywhere in the heart of humanity arise as inspiration back in each individual heart. As we live from our hearts, we change the atmosphere in our homes and groups, and this contributes to building a culture of the heart in the world.

The culture of the heart is a shift from the culture of the mind and it is already forming; we see a greater acceptance of the differences of others, more consideration for the needs of others, an emphasis on seeking happiness, and an acknowledgment of an emotional wisdom that surpasses mental intelligence, occurring in education, in business, and in government. Alongside these advances, there are many examples of the opposite, but this is to be expected in a transition period. Inevitably, the approach of the heart will increase because it results in better health, increased creativity, greater productivity, and greater adaptability to change. In short, it works better and feels better.

The heart integrates all parts of the self and so it can create physical health from emotional and spiritual health. A strong heart welcomes change and stress. The heart is inclusive, so society can benefit from all its contributors. The heart also embraces diversity as an exploration of our hidden potentials. Furthermore, it is the Spirit of Guidance speaking through our hearts that guides the evolution of humanity.

How can the Culture of the Heart be developed? The practice for developing the Culture of the Heart has four steps. These steps are being practiced by millions already, and the more conscious we are about this practice the sooner the culture shift will occur.

1. Think of your physical heart as you breathe in and out.
2. Think of the people present around you.
   Recognize and acknowledge the specific greatness in each person.
   Accept their vision of your greatness.
   Respect the sensitivity of each person's heart.
   Think of and speak to each person with delicacy and sympathy.
3. Think of the feelings, needs and greatness of those not present:
   your family and friends,
   other people you know, and
   people you know of through connections and media.
4. Finally, recognize that your feeling for others is the emotion of the Heart of Humanity for itself.
   Every impulse of love that rises in your heart is the action of the love in the Heart of Humanity.
   Love is guiding you toward the purpose of your life.

Today there are nearly seven billion people on the planet, and through global communication they have more effect upon each other than ever before. In the past year, for example, people around the world applauded when an unknown, older woman opened her mouth to sing and aston ished an English TV talent show, and people around the world grieved when a liberal politician was shot by a mentally-disturbed gunmen in our home state of Arizona, USA. In one Mayan, astronomical cycle of 26,000 years, the world has gone from the stone age to globalization. Human creativity and innovation is boundless, and as we stand at the transition to a new cycle, we have the potential to build a common ideal.

Only the message of the heart can overcome the fear and

pessimism that is gripping the world today, a result of not appreciating the beauty and interconnection of all life. Humanity will overcome the ecological, political, economic and religious tensions of the present culture of the mind, and thrive in the next 26,000-year cycle, by collectively taking the next step into Stage Two, the stage of the culture of the heart, and Stage Three, the unity of the family of humanity.

The message of the heart will guide humanity, but it needs to come through the heart so that each human being receives it. It cannot be based on any one prophet; it must be delivered to each community by one of its own. The attainment of illumination and a coordination of illuminated souls worldwide will be needed to help humankind find the ideal within their hearts and to demonstrate commitment to that ideal, of love, harmony and beauty.

Many representatives of the heart are needed to deliver its message from heart to heart. Anyone with the realization of Step Four or greater can help. Truly, one person with the realization of the heart can have an effect upon thousands, and one person with the realization of unity can have an effect on the whole of humanity.

Appendices

1. The Parable of the Bull

Written by the Chinese Master Kakuan in the 12th century, the Parable of the Bull provides a description of the Steps of the Path from the Buddhist tradition. It became widely-known in the west by its inclusion in the book *Zen Flesh, Zen Bones,* a wonderful book which introduced the Zen Buddhist tradition to the west. One of the editors and translators who produced the book, Paul Reps, was a student of Hazrat Inayat Khan.[89]

The 10 bull drawings are correlated with the steps of The Map.

1. In Search of the Bull
(aimless searching, only the sound of cicadas)
Step 1, Commitment: the work has been started.

2. Discovery of the Footprints
(a path to follow)
Step 2, Testing: The existence of the bull is confirmed by the footprints. Thus the commitment is tested and confirmed.

3. Perceiving the Bull
(but only its rear, not its head)
Step 3, Harmony: The bull is found. The scenery is pleasant. The most important part of the bull is not seen. End of first stage.

4. Catching the Bull
(a great struggle, the bull repeatedly escapes, discipline required)
Step 4, Idealization: The discovery of the heart allows the mind to

[89] Reps (1998).

be tamed and held.

5. Taming the Bull

(less straying, less discipline, bull becomes gentle and obedient)

Step 5, Expertise: The power of the heart is harnessed.

6. Riding the Bull Home

(great joy. "I direct the endless rhythm. Whoever hears this melody will join me.")

Step 5, Expertise: Enjoying success and leadership, fame spreads.

7. The Bull Transcended

("I reach home. I am serene. The bull too can rest. In blissful repose, I have abandoned the whip and rope.")

Step 6, Unlearning: abandoning the tools, ending the struggle, withdrawing from conflict. Passive.

8. Both Bull and Self Transcended

("Person and bull — all merge in no-thing. This heaven is so vast.")

Step 7, Unity: The Bull and Self are One. The vastness of unity.

9. Reaching the Source

("Dwelling in one's true abode, unconcerned with that without. From the beginning, truth is clear.")

Step 8, Guidance: Guidance makes the truth clear. Inner direction requires withdrawal.

10. Return to Society

("I mingle with the people of the world. The dead trees become alive. Everyone I look upon becomes enlightened.")

Step 9, Illumination: Radiating light to others.

2. The Conference of the Birds

Farid-ud-din Attar wrote an allegory of the spiritual path in the year 1177. Titled "The Conference of the Birds", it tells the story of a large group of birds who set out to find the king of the birds, called the *Simorgh*. Only 30 of the birds complete the journey, finding themselves gazing into a crystal lake at their own reflection. In Persian, the phrase "si morgh" means "30 birds". In the story the birds pass through Seven Valleys, which we relate to the steps of the Map as follows.

The Seven Valleys	The Map
1. The Valley of the Quest	Steps 1, Commitment, and 2, Testing.
2. The Valley of Love and Devotion	Step 4, Idealization. The heart's opening, beyond the Harmony of step 3.
3. The Valley of Knowledge Which Illuminates	Step 5, Expertise. This knowledge comes from the integration of one's ideal and reason.
4. The Valley of Annihilation	Step 6, Unlearning
5. The Valley of Unity	Step 7, Unity
6. The Valley of Amazement, seeing the Beloved in everyone and the cause behind the cause.	Step 8, Guidance. Communicating with the Beloved to understand Her wishes.
7. The Valley of the Realization of God. The peace that every soul is seeking.	Step 9, Illumination

3: Phrases for Each Step

These phrases were given by Hazrat Inayat Khan to his students as meditation practices. A phrase can be studied, repeated silently while breathing consciously, and observed in its effect in life. We have arranged them into the steps of realization to transmit the feeling of each step.

Step 1

Initiation is a step in a direction one does not know.

In seeking the spiritual path I am sought after by the spirit.

Step 2

All situations of life are tests to bring out the real and the false.

To be really sorry for one's errors is like opening the door of heaven.

I draw all my strength from my humility.

Be firm in faith through life's tests and trials.

Gold is that which proves to be real to the end of the test.

Step 3

My life is changing and taking a better turn.

Endurance makes things precious and people great.

Leave all that unsaid which, by being said, creates inharmony.

Understanding gives one harmony in the home and peace outside the home; it is understanding which gives a person riches.

It does not matter how hard I work, it's what I accomplish that counts.

Step 4

To discover the heart is the greatest initiation.

In all directions of progress my ideal is the compass that shows the way.

Happiness lies in thinking or doing that which one considers beautiful.

O beloved ideal of my soul, pray show thyself to me in human guise.

Open the door to the temple of my heart, so I may perceive God through each person.

Step 5

Let me own my own self, O lord, that I can call something my own in this world.

The human heart is the home of the soul, and upon this home the comfort and power of the soul depend.

It is with Thy might alone that I can lift up life's responsibilities.

May my life become powerful and harmonious.

Success is my birthright.

My mind is still, my thought is steady, my sight is keen, my life is balanced.

Think of the Beloved, consider what the beloved needs and wants.

Step 6

The real learning is unlearning all one has learned.

I am not but a wave rising in Thy heart.

In the light I behold Thy beauty, Beloved; through the darkness Thy mystery is revealed to my heart.

Lift the barrier, Lord, that divides Thee from me.

My lifelong sorrow I forget when Thou castest Thy glance upon me.

O nature sublime, in thy silence I hear thy mournful cry.

The pain of life is the price paid for the quickening of the heart.

Thou teachest me patience, sublime nature, by thy patient waiting.

Thou wilt guide me aright, Lord; I am a child on life's path.

Step 7

The clouds of doubt and fear are scattered by Thy piercing glance.

All ignorance vanishes in Thy illuminating presence.

As invisible as space, as inconceivable as time, is Thy being, O Lord.

God is love; when love is awakened in the heart, God is awakened there.

Since my soul has caught Thy light, my glance has become a comet.

Since Thy joyful smile has produced a new light in my heart, I see the sun shine everywhere.

Sublime nature, thy reflection produces in my heart God's glorious vision.

Step 8

I hear, Lord, Thy speechless call in the sublimity of nature.

Silent voice, in the stillness of night I hear thy whisper.

O Spirit of Guidance, throw Thy divine light on my path.

Speak to me from within, my Lord; the ears of Thy servant are listening.

Speak to me, my Lord, through the words of Thy Messenger.

Speak, Lord, in the stillness of nature; my heart's ears are open to hear Thy call.

My self, how wonderful it is to feel that if no one in the world understood me, still you would understand.

Step 9

Let Thy sun shine in my heart.

My heart is Thy sacred shrine.

Thou art closer to me than my self.

My thoughtful self, Bear all and do nothing, Hear all and say nothing, Give all and take nothing, Serve all and be nothing.

Wide horizon, thou makest my heart wide as thyself.

I consider my action towards every person as my action towards God; and the action of every person towards me I take as an action of God.

Let Thy word, God, become my life's expression.

The consciousness of unity is life's culmination.

Step 10

Help me to serve Thy cause.

Let Thy servant, O Lord, be my Master.

Man's greatest privilege is to become a suitable instrument of God.

References

Al-Sarraj, Abu Nasr and Reynold Nicholson. (2010) *The Kitáb al-luma' fi'l-Tasawwuf of Abú Nasr 'abdallah b. 'Ali al-Sarráj al-Tusi*. Nabu Press.

Anderson, Clifford. (1995) *The Stages of Life*. New York: Atlantic Monthly Press.

Attar, Farid-ud-din. (2003) *The Conference of the Birds*. Interlink Books.

Bair, Puran (2007) "Visible Light Radiated from the Heart with Heart Rhythm Meditation". *Subtle Energies and Energy Medicine*. 16(3): 211-215

Bair, Puran, and Susanna Bair. (2007) *Energize Your Heart In Four Dimensions*. Tucson, AZ: Living Heart Media.

—. (2010) *Living from the Heart: Heart Rhythm Meditation for Energy, Clarity, Peace, and Inner Power*. Tucson, AZ: Living Heart Media.

Barks, Coleman, trans. (1995) *The Essential Rumi*. San Francisco: Harper.

Bly, Robert (2005). *The Winged Energy of Delight: Selected Poems*. New york: Harper Perennial.

Bryant, Edwin F. (2009) *The Yoga Sutras of Patanjali: A New Edition, Translation, and Commentary*. North Point Press.

Carter, John Ross, trans., Mahinda Palihawadana, trans. (2008) *The Dhammapada: The Sayings of the Buddha*. London: Oxford University Press.

Dass, Ram. (1971) *Be Here Now.* New Mexico: The Lama Foundation.

Erikson, Erik H. (1994) *Identity and the Life Cycle.* New York: W.W. Norton & Co.

Fletcher, P.C., O. Zafiris, C.D. Frith, R.A.E. Honey, P.R. Corlett, K. Zilles, and G.R. Fink. (2005) "On the Benefits of not Trying: Brain Activity and Connectivity Reflecting the Interactions of Explicit and Implicit Sequence Learning". *Cerebral Cortex* 2005 15(7): 1002-1015; doi: 10.1093/cercor/bhh201

Gladwell, Malcolm. (2009) *What the Dog Saw and Other Adventures.* New York: Little, Brown, and Co.

Hitchens, Christopher. (2007) *God Is Not Great: How Religion Poisons Everything.* New York: Twelve Books.

Jung, C.J. (1981) *The Archetypes and the Collective Unconscious.* Princeton, NJ: Princeton University Press.

Khan, Inayat. *Complete Works.* www.hazrat-inayat-khan.org

—. (1960-64) *The Sufi Message of Hazrat Inayat Khan, Volumes 1-13.* London: Barrie and Rockcliff.

—. (1978) *The Complete Sayings of Hazrat Inayat Khan.* New Lebanon, NY: Omega Publications.

—. (1980) Tales Told by Hazrat Inayat Khan. New Lebanon, New York: Sufi Order Publications.

—. (1989) *Complete Works of Pir-o-Murshid Hazrat Inayat Khan, Original Texts: Lectures on Sufism, 1923 I: January-June.* London/The Hague: East-West Publications.

—. (1990) *Complete Works of Pir-o-Murshid Hazrat Inayat Khan, Original Texts: Lectures on Sufism, 1922 I: January-August.* London / The Hague: East-West Publications.

—. *Esoteric Papers* (unpublished).

Khan, Vilayat Inayat. (1974) *Toward the One.* New York: Harper and Row.

—. (1978) *The Message of Our Time: The Life and Teachings of the Sufi Master Pir-o-Murshid Hazrat Inayat Khan.* San Francisco: Harper and Row.

—. (1982) *Introducing Spirituality into Counseling and Therapy.* New Lebanon, NY: Omega Publications.

—. (1983) *Retreat Manual.* Unpublished manuscript.

—. (1988) *Rehearsal for Life.* Unpublished manuscript.

—. (1992) *The Call of the Dervish: Breakthrough In Spiritual Realization.* New Lebanon, NY: Omega Publications.

—. (1994) *That Which Transpires Behind That Which Appears.* New Lebanon, NY: Omega Publications.

—. (1996) *Tools of Meditation.* Seattle: Sufi Order International.

—. (2000) *Awakening: A Sufi Experience.* New York: Tarcher.

—. (2003) *In Search of the Hidden Treasure.* New York: Tarcher.

Khusro, Amir. Khalid Shaida, trans. (2008) *Khusro, the Indian Orpheus: A Hundred Odes.* BookSurge Publishing.

Kotsonis, John K. (2007) *An Orthodox Christian Study on Unceasing Prayer*. Theandros. 4: 3. www.theandros.com

Levinson, Daniel J. (1986) *The Seasons of A Man's Life*. New York: Ballantine.

Logothetis, Spyridon. (1982) *The Heart: An Orthodox Christian Spiritual Guide*. Holy Transfiguration Monastery, 1982

Massignon, Louis. Herbert Mason, trans. (1994) *Hallaj: Mystic and Martyr*. Princeton, NJ: Princeton University Press.

Millman, Dan. (2006) *Way of the Peaceful Warrior*. New York: HJ Kramer.

Nicholson, Reynold A., ed. (1898) *Selected Poems from the Divani Shamsi Tabriz*. London: Cambridge University Press.

Osborn, Eric. (2008) *Clement of Alexandria*. London: Cambridge University Press.

Reps, Paul, and Nyogen Sanzaki, trans. (1998) *Zen Flesh, Zen Bones*. Tuttle Press. First published, 1957.

Smith, John D., trans. (2009) *The Mahabharata*. New York: Penguin Classics.

Taleb, Nassim. (2010) *The Black Swan: The Impact of the Highly Improbable*. 2nd ed. New York: Random House.

The INSTITUTE *for* APPLIED MEDITATION

Join the Institute for Applied Meditation Mailing List and we will send you a **free meditation CD**! We never share our list with anyone. You can unsubscribe at any time. *The starred fields are required.

☐ Mr. ☐ Ms.

* Last * First

* Email

* Address

* City

* State * Zip

* Country * Phone

Comments: please tell us about yourself

I want to use Heart Rhythm Meditation to help me with:

☐ Stress reduction
☐ High blood pressure
☐ Sleeping better
☐ Anxiety
☐ Heart disease
☐ General physical health
☐ General mental health
☐ Relationships
☐ Career
☐ Emotional growth
☐ Spiritual connection

Send to PO Box 86149, Tucson, AZ 85754, or fill out the form online at IAMheart.org.

I remember . . . my purpose.

I am to assist others to the next step, the next phase, the next plane.

I am to create images of the ancient hills, other planes, spiritual planes.

I am to live by the desert where the vibrations are such that one is in multiple planes simultaneously.

I am to follow the heart path and love completely and unconditionally.